Wildflowers
of Tidewater Virginia

Wildflowers

of Tidewater Virginia

Oscar W. Gupton and Fred C. Swope
Department of Biology
Virginia Military Institute

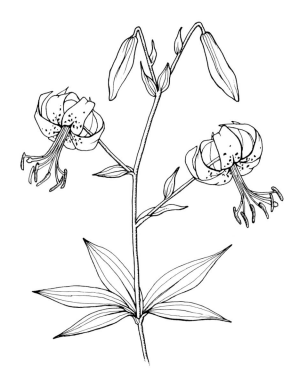

University Press of Virginia

Charlottesville

THE UNIVERSITY PRESS OF VIRGINIA
Copyright © 1982 by the Rector and Visitors
of the University of Virginia

First published 1982

Library of Congress Cataloging in Publication Data
Gupton, Oscar W.
  Wildflowers of tidewater Virginia.

  Includes indexes.
    1. Wild flowers—Virginia—Identification.
I. Swope, Fred C. II. Title. III. Title: Tide-
water Virginia.
QK191.G893   582.13'09755'1   81–16247
ISBN 0–8139–0922–8   AACR2

Printed in the United States of America

To

Mae and Marguerite

Contents

Introduction

Walking among the wildflowers of tidewater Virginia brings the pleasure that always accompanies any sort of exploration of nature; however, the reward in this instance is twofold, because the plants here are a part of the setting in which were played out so many of the crucial scenes that culminated in the emergence of a new nation. The varied floral displays that grace the banks of the rivers Potomac, Rappahannock, York, and James lend their fragrance to the breezes blowing over soils that once were a part of the dooryards of the first permanent English settlement at Jamestown. The colors of the blossoms at Yorktown are reminiscent of the flags, the uniforms, and the blood that in earlier times colored the battlefield upon which Cornwallis surrendered, and their beauty enhances that of the thoroughfares trodden by so many historic figures in the old colonial capital of Williamsburg.

The species of plants considered herein are plants of the coastal plain with the inclusion of a very few species that are limited to the western or inland border called the fall zone. For the most part these plants are not difficult to find, since they are abundant and distributed generally. There are some, though, that are plentiful where found but are noted only in particular sites, and still others that are scarce throughout. Many of these plants, as far as is known, originated here, and others were brought in accidentally or intentionally from other countries or other parts of this country and have maintained themselves in this flora. A few of these wildflowers can be seen only in places where disturbance has been at a minimum, but most of them can be readily observed along the borders of the roads that traverse the woods, fields, and thickets.

This vast network of roads that provide us the opportunity to view in a short time and with little difficulty so many of the diverse elements of the vegetation is greatly appreciated for its many benefits; nevertheless, these implements of easy access should also serve as a tocsin to make us ever mindful of the enormous measure by which we disturb that portion of the earth so necessary for plant growth and consequently pay the price of things natural. Growing concern over environmental problems has brought the terms *ecology*, *preservation*, and *conservation* into general and frequent use and turned our thoughts toward contemplation of the possible impact of the actions of today on the landscapes of tomorrow.

The plant world, upon which the very existence of mankind is dependent, is such a highly visible and aesthetically appealing product of the land and so much affected by human activities that a better acquaintance with it must surely result in sharpening the awareness of many of the problems and strengthening the resolve to make wiser decisions in the use of natural resources. Familiarity with the names of some of the botanical residents of the national birthplace should help to make us more alive to the circumstances in which they exist.

The design of this book is to furnish information with which the plants can be identified without resorting to technical language or requiring that the structure of plant parts be understood. Color photographs and descriptive comments are provided as identification materials for each species. The photographs were taken in the field under natural light conditions, and there is a notation of the size of the photograph relative to the actual size of the plant. The descriptions are self-contained and have no reference to any included diagrams or glossary.

There are photographs of 200 species that are mostly herbaceous but include a few woody vines and shrubs. These photographed species represent 165 genera and 67 families, and there are 300 citations of additional species that include comments to aid in their recognition. This is a guide, then, to 500 species of plants in the tidewater of Virginia, and since the plants range in one or more directions far outside the borders of this area, the guide is applicable on a much wider scale.

We are grateful for the support of the Research Committee of the Virginia Military Institute.

Oscar W. Gupton

Fred C. Swope

Lexington, Virginia

Format

The plants are divided into groups according to flower color or, in a very few instances, fruit color. There are eight groups arranged in the following order: green, white, yellow, orange, red, pink, blue, and purple.

There is a color tab provided at the edge of each page.

The species comprising each of the color groups are placed in order of the time of flowering or, rarely, fruiting.

The size of the photograph relative to the actual size of the plant is indicated by a magnification symbol. The symbol $\times 2$, for example, means that the size of the photograph is twice that of the plant; $\times 1$ means that the photograph is the same size as the plant; and $\times \frac{1}{2}$ means that the photograph is one half the size of the plant.

The text accompanying each photograph consists of the following information which is given in the order indicated throughout:

Common name of species
Scientific name of species   Flowering period

Description:

Size of the plant is indicated by a statement of the approximate overall height.

Leaf character is given by reference to size, shape, number, arrangement, texture, or other quality peculiar to the plant.

Flower character is cited with respect to those features indicated for the leaf, and any variations in color pattern are included.

Fruit character is sometimes noted as for the leaf and flower.

Other species, usually of the same genus, similar to the pictured species are indicated by scientific name and accompanied by brief mention of distinguishing features.

Medicinal or food uses of the plant are stated.

Toxic properties attributed to the species are given if

sickness or death has been reported from eating or if skin inflammation has resulted from handling. This information is included whether humans or other animals are affected.

Miscellaneous comments of general interest in other categories may be included.

An additional common name for the plant may be given.

Habitat or type of environment in which the plant is usually found is noted. The costal plain is delineated on the map on page xiii.

The scientific names follow the eighth edition of *Gray's Manual of Botany*, and an index to the families to which the species belong along with a guide to the pronunciation of scientific names is provided.

The works listed below are plant manuals with keys consisting of technical information for identification of the plants of the northeastern United States.

Fernald, M. L. 1950. *Gray's Manual of Botany*. Eighth edition. American Book Company.

Gleason, M. A. 1952 *Illustrated Flora of the Northeastern United States and Adjacent Canada*. The New York Botanical Garden.

Gleason, M. A., and A. Cronquist. 1963 *Manual of the Vascular Plants of Northeastern United States and Adjacent Canada*. D. Van Nostrand Company.

Rickett, N. W. 1953. *Wildflowers of the United States*. Crown Publishers.

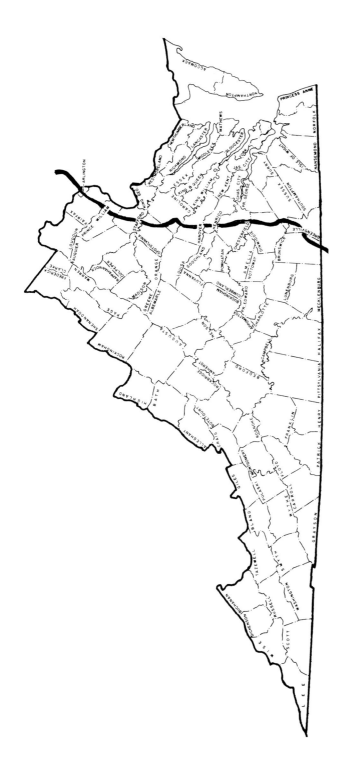

Coastal Plain
(Tidewater)

Wildflowers
of Tidewater Virginia

Virginia Creeper

× ⅔

Parthenocissus quinquefolia June–July

The stems of this climbing vine have curling tendrils with adhesive disks at the ends. The long-stalked leaves are divided into usually 5 segments 2 to 6 inches long and toothed toward the tip. The flowers are very small and grow in large purple-stalked clusters. Flower color is greenish white, yellowish white, or yellowish green. The fruits are dark blue to black berries about ¼ to ½ inch in diameter. The leaves turn bright red in autumn, and the plant is widely used, usually along walls or fences, as an ornamental. Woodbine is another name for this species. *Dry or moist woods.*

Green Fringed Orchid × 1

Habenaria lacera June–August

This orchid may stand 8 inches to over 2½ feet tall. The narrow, pointed leaves are 3 to 8 inches long. The pale green or yellow, fringed flowers are about ½ inch long. Flower color may vary from white to greenish brown. Flower clusters are 2 to 10 inches long. *H. ciliaris*, another species with fringed flowers, is included here, and an additional species is cited in the description of *H. clavellata*. Green Fringed Orchid is also called Ragged Orchis. *Wet woods and meadows, bogs, marshes.*

Wood Orchid

×1

Habenaria clavellata   June–August

This orchid is 4 inches to 1½ feet tall. There is usually 1 leaf 2 to 7 inches long midway up the stem, and any additional leaves are extremely small. The very small flowers are less than ½ inch across and range in color from white to greenish yellow. *H. flava* may superficially resemble the Wood Orchid in flower size and color, but 2, 3, or more leaves are present, and leafy projections from beneath the flowers are conspicuous. Two other species, *H. lacera* and *H. ciliaris*, are included here. A second name for Wood Orchid is Club-spur Orchid. *Bogs, wet woods, and meadows.*

Sweet Rush

× ½

Cyperus retrofractus   July–September

This sedge is 8 inches to 2½ feet tall, and the stems are usually triangular and smooth. The grasslike leaves are long and narrow. The very small flowers are enclosed in a series of flat, overlapping scales arranged in dense clusters so that they point downward. The flower clusters are at the tips of smooth stalks of varying lengths. Although the many sedge species are often difficult to separate, there are 2 species similar to this one. *C. plukenetii* and *C. dipsaciformis* have rough stems, and the former also has rough flowering stalks with leaves at the stalk bases shorter than the longest stalk, while the latter has smooth flowering stalks and leaves longer than the longest flowering stalk. Sweet Rush is also called Galingale. *Dry and sandy soil.*

5

Sandspur × 1¼

Cenchrus tribuloides July–October

The widely branching and sometimes reclining stems are 8 inches to 2 feet long. The leaves are those typical of grasses, narrow, pointed, and sheathing the stem. The very small flowers are completely enclosed within a spiny burr. The spines are flattened, densely hairy at base, and ¼ inch or more long. These burrs later turn from green to reddish brown. *C. incertus* and *C. pauciflorus* have burrs not so densely hairy with spines usually less than ¼ inch long. The former has burrs with 6 to 10 spines, while the latter has burrs with less than 10 spines. The cluster of spines can inflict painful puncture wounds on bare feet. These plants are also called Burgrass. *Dunes, sandy roadsides, and fields.*

Bloodroot

× ½

Sanguinaria canadensis   March–April

The plant attains a height of from 2 to 15 inches. There is usually a single variously lobed leaf 2 to 8 inches in diameter folded around the flower stalk. The solitary flower has 7 to 12 petals and is usually white but infrequently flushed with pink. The fruit is 1½ to 2½ inches long and more or less pointed at each end. The red sap of the plant has been used as a dye; it is poisonous and a skin irritant. Red Puccoon is another name given to this species. *Open woods, roadside banks.*

May-apple × ½

Podophyllum peltatum   March–June

Height of the plant is about ½ foot to 1½ feet. The round, umbrellalike leaves are 5 to 13 inches in diameter and divided into several lobes. There is one flower, 1 inch to 2 inches in diameter, situated between two leaves. The yellow fruit is 1½ to 2 inches long and edible when ripe. Unripe fruits and much of the rest of the plant are poisonous, and the underground parts in particular may cause skin irritation upon handling. This species frequently occurs in large, dense colonies. Another common name is Mandrake. *Moist woods, roadsides, meadows.*

Spring Cress

× 1¼

Cardamine bulbosa   March–June

The slender stems are 6 inches to about 2 feet tall with several bulblike underground parts. Basal leaves are round with long stalks, while higher stem leaves are narrowed, often toothed, and stalkless or very short-stalked. The white, 4-petaled flowers are about an inch across and form a cross. Fruits are very slender pods. *C. douglassii* is very similar with pink or purple flowers. Three other white-flowered species have highly segmented leaves. *C. hirsuta* has many basal leaves and hairy lower leaf stalks. *C. parviflora*, of dry soils, has leaves ½ to 1 inch long. *C. pensylvanica*, of wet soils, has leaves 1¼ to 3½ inches long. *Wet woods or meadows, shallow water.*

Trillium   × 1

Trillium pusillum   April

This rare trillium is 2 inches to about a foot tall. There are 3 leaves an inch to 3 inches long, narrowed at both ends, and stalkless or nearly so that encircle the stem just beneath the flower. The solitary flower is white to pink, about an inch to 1½ inches across, and stalkless or very short-stalked. This is the only trillium of the coastal plain, although *T. sessile*, a larger plant with mottled leaves and maroon flowers, grows along its western border. The 3 leaves and 3-parted flowers give the plant its name. *Low and wet woods*.

Star-of-Bethlehem

× ¾

Ornithogalum umbellatum   April–May

This plant is about 5 inches to over a foot tall. The narrow, grasslike leaves are pointed and long, some of them usually overtopping the flowers. The flowers are about 1 to 2 inches across and grow in broad, loose clusters. Each flower has 6 spreading, pointed segments that are white above and green or green-striped beneath. This plant was introduced from Europe for ornamental purposes and has escaped cultivation into our flora. The species is poisonous, which seems to make its other name, Nap at Noon, a better fit than Star of Bethlehem. *Roadsides, fields, lawns, streamsides.*

11

Corn Salad

× 1

Valerianella radiata   April–May

The stems of this plant fork repeatedly and are 6 inches to over 2 feet tall. The paired leaves are an inch to 3 inches long, stalkless, and oblong with the widest part often nearer the tip and usually a few teeth near the base. The tiny flowers are usually about 1/16 inch long and white and grow in dense clusters at the ends of the stems. Two other species, *V. olitoria* and *V. umbilicata*, are similar, but the former has pale blue flowers, and the latter has flowers about twice as long and less densely clustered. Another name for these plants is Lamb's Lettuce. *Roadsides, fields, and wood borders.*

12

Atamasco Lily   × 1

Zephranthes atamasco   April–May

The leafless flowering stalk of this plant grows from a bulb
and is 6 inches to more than a foot tall. The narrow, pointed
leaves arise from the base of the plant and are 6 inches to
nearly 1½ feet long and usually less than ½ inch wide. The
single flower is white or occasionally pink-tinted and 2 to 4
inches across. The leaves and especially the bulbs of this
species have been reported as poisonous. This plant is also
known as Rain Lily, in reference, according to some, to the
populous colonies often seen after early spring showers. *Moist
woods and wood borders, moist meadows.*

13

Wood Anemone

× ¾

Anemone quinquefolia   April–June

The plant stands 2 inches to about a foot tall. There is usually
a single long-stalked leaf from the base of the stem and a pair
or circle of 3 leaves a little distance beneath the flower. Each
leaf is divided into 3 segments that are toothed and frequently
lobed, the lateral segment often so deeply as to appear to be
separate segments. The solitary flower is white or sometimes
pinkish and ½ inch to 2 inches across. Another species, *A.
virginiana*, is also cited here. The anemones are also called by
the name Windflower. *Moist woods, wood borders.*

14

Japanese Honeysuckle

Lonicera japonica   April–July

The climbing or trailing stems of this plant are usually densely tangled. The evergreen leaves are an inch to 3 inches long and taper to a pointed or rounded tip. Leaf margins are usually without lobes or teeth, but occasionally they will be present. The fragrant flowers are an inch to 2 inches long and vary in color from white to cream, pink, or reddish purple. The fruits are black, shiny, and round. *L. sempervirens* has 1 or 2 pairs of upper leaves fused at their bases and tubular red or yellow flowers an inch to 2 inches long. Japanese Honeysuckle is an Asian species that reminds us of the potential danger of introducing a life form to a foreign environment where natural factors of growth control may not exist. *Woods, fields, roadsides, pastures.*

Devil's Bit

× ½

Chamaelirium luteum   May–June

This plant stands a foot to over 2 feet tall. The larger basal leaves are 3 to 6 inches long, oval to nearly round, and much wider near the tip, while the upper leaves are smaller and narrower. This plant is a male in which the very small white flowers are clustered on a slender, usually drooping, stalk that is also white. The female flowering cluster is shorter and thicker, ending in a blunt tip. Fairy Wand is another name for this plant. *Moist woods*.

Wineberry

× 1¾

Rubus phoenicolasius   May–June

The stems are as much as 6 feet tall and are covered with a dense growth of reddish purple bristles and scattered thorns. The leaves are divided into 3 segments that are oval, toothed, and white on the underside. The flowers are an inch or more across and appear as green stars with a white center. The flower stalks and the basal part of the flowers are covered with sticky, reddish purple bristles. The fruits are red, about ½ inch in diameter, and edible. The foliage, reddish purple bristles, and tart fruits, cited for preserving and eating, make this an attractive plant. It is also named Wine Raspberry. *Open woods, wood borders, roadsides.*   19

Zenobia × ¾

Zenobia pulverulenta May–June

This is a rare shrub that stands 3 to 6 feet tall. The stems
sometimes have a white or bluish coating that will rub off.
The leaves are 1½ to 3 inches long, ½ inch to 2 inches wide,
rounded or pointed at both ends, and green or bluish white
underneath. The flowers are about ½ inch long and wide
with short, broad lobes that are folded back at the tips, and
the clusters are elongate and 4 inches to over a foot long. The
fruits are about ¼ inch long, rounded at the base, and flattened on top. This is a handsome shrub of wet soils. *Swamps,
bogs, wet wood borders.*

Partridge Berry

× 1¼

Mitchella repens   May–July

The stems of this plant lie on the ground, rooted where leaves
are produced, and form extensive mats. The evergreen leaves
are paired, nearly round, and dark green with pale green to
almost white veining. The flowers are white, occasionally
pink-tinged, hairy, and grow in pairs. The fruits are bright
red berries about ½ inch or less in diameter and result from
the fusion of the paired flowers. Partridge Berry is also called
Running Box. *Rich woods, streamsides.*

21

White Milkweed

×1

Asclepias variegata   May–July

This milkweed is 8 inches to almost 4 feet tall. The paired leaves are 2 to 5 inches long and oblong with blunt or rounded tips. The flowers are bright white, occasionally pink-tinged, with a purple center. There are 3 additional species that have white flowers, but the white has a greenish cast. *A. verticillata* has numerous narrow leaves in circles. *A. exaltata* has flowers with conspicuous curved horns on top and erect stems 2½ to 5 feet tall. *A. viridiflora* has flowers usually more green than white and stems a foot to 2½ feet tall and often leaning. *Woods, wood borders.*

22

White Campion

× ½

Lychnis alba   May–August

The stems are hairy and grow 1½ to 4 feet tall. The paired leaves are stalkless, an inch to 6 inches long, and taper to a pointed or rounded tip. The flowers are white or occasionally pink, about an inch across, and have notched or cleft petals. *Silene noctiflora* is very similar to White Campion, but the bracts, or very small leaves, just below the flowers are very narrow and nearly straight, while in White Campion they are short and rounded. *L. coronaria*, a red-flowered species, is included here. There are stories of the varied misfortunes that have befallen those who pick the campions. *Roadsides, fields.*

23

Daisy Fleabane

× 1¾

Erigeron strigosus   May–September

The slender stems are a foot to 4 feet tall. The leaves are narrow, mostly less than ½ inch wide, often wider near the tip, and have few or no teeth. The tiny flowers are clustered so as to resemble a single flower about an inch across with a yellow center, white border, and very narrow and numerous petals. *E. annuus* is very similar, but the leaves are mostly wider and have conspicuous teeth. *E. vernus* is usually a smaller plant with very few leaves and flower heads with fewer "petals." Other species are cited in the description of *E. pulchellus. Roadsides, fields, wood borders, pastures.*

Alligator Weed

Alternanthera philoxeroides   May–September

The trailing, densely crowded stems may form extensive
mats. The paired leaves are well spaced on the stem, an inch
to 4 inches long, oblong, and usually wider near the tip. The
whitish clusters of very small flowers are about ½ inch across
and are at the end of a stalk ½ inch to almost 3 inches long.
A. achyrantha is somewhat similar, but it has much larger,
more oval leaves and stalkless flower clusters, and it is found
on dry soils. Alligator Weed can be to the water what Japanese Honeysuckle is to the land, rigorously choking out other
forms of plant life. *Water or very wet soil.*

Spring Ladies' Tresses

× 1⅓

Spiranthes vernalis   May–September

This orchid is 8 inches to 4 feet tall, and the upper parts are densely covered with short hairs. Leaves at base and on the lower stem are 2 to 8 inches long and narrow and sheath the stem. The white or cream flowers are arranged in a spiral. *S. praecox* is similar but has few or no hairs and leaves usually less than ¼ inch wide. *S. cernua* and *S. ovalis* have flowers in more than one spiral, and the former has downturned flowers about ½ inch long, while the latter has flowers about ¼ inch long and leaves much wider near the tip. *S. grayi* and *S. gracilis* are very slender with stalked, nonsheathing leaves, but the former has flowers less than ¼ inch long and withered leaves about ¼ inch wide, while the latter has flowers almost ½ inch long and leaves ¾ to 1 inch wide often present at flowering. *Marshes, dry or moist sandy soils.*

26

White Sweet Clover

$\times \frac{1}{3}$

Melilotus alba

May–October

This plant is 3 to nearly 10 feet tall. The leaves are divided into 3 segments that are oblong, sometimes wider near the tip, and about ½ to 1 inch long. The white flowers are only about ¼ inch long and grow in slender clusters 2 to 8 inches long. There is one other species, *M. officinalis*, that is very similar but is usually not so tall and has slightly larger yellow flowers. Both of these species of sweet clover are used for making hay. Proper curing is essential to prevent the production of a poisonous substance. White Melilot is another name for White Sweet Clover. *Fields, roadsides.*

27

Poison Hemlock

× ¼

Conium maculatum June–July

This freely and widely branching plant may be 4 to 10 feet tall. The stems are hollow and usually spotted with purple or red. Leaves are divided into segments which are in turn divided into smaller lobed segments. The tiny white flowers are in large clusters made up of smaller similar clusters in which the individual flower stalks all arise from the same point. Encircling the base of the flower clusters are small, narrow, and pointed leaves with a green stripe. *Cicuta maculata* is somewhat similar but has no striped leaves around the large flower cluster and has pointed, toothed leaf segments. Both of these species are very poisonous. Poison Hemlock is said to have been the instrument of Socrates' death. *Roadsides, fields, moist to dry wood borders.*

Thimbleweed

Anemone virginiana   June–July

Thimbleweed stems are a foot to nearly 3 feet tall. The large leaves are almost round in outline and divided into 3 or 5 segments that are toothed and often lobed. There are leaves from the base of the stem with very long stalks and a circle of 3 leaves higher on the stem. The long flower stalks usually have a pair of smaller leaves and a single flower. The flower color is white or greenish to yellowish and occasionally pinkish. The fruits form a cylinder about an inch long and ½ inch thick. Another species, *A. quinquefolia*, is cited. Windflower is another name for these species. *Open woods, wood borders.*

Long-leaved Summer Bluets

× 2¼

Houstonia longifolia

June–August

The slender stems are 4 inches to nearly a foot tall and are usually freely branching. The paired, narrow leaves are ½ inch to 1½ inches long, ¼ inch or less wide, and narrowed to the base. The small flowers are less than ½ inch long and are pale purple to white. Flower clusters are at or near the top of the plant. This species and two others are very similar. *H. lanceolata* has leaves about ½ inch or more wide that are rounded at the base. *H. tenuifolia* has leaves barely ⅛ inch wide, narrowed to the base, and purple flowers. These species and *H. purpurea*, cited in the description of *H. caerulea*, are frequently not clearly distinguished. *Dry and rocky soil.*

Culver's Root

× ½

Veronicastrum virginicum   June–August

This infrequent species is slender and 2½ to 6 feet tall. The leaves grow in circles and are 2 to 6 inches long, toothed, and taper gradually to a point. The small white flowers grow in slender, pointed clusters at the top of the stem. The stamens, or pollen-bearing organs, give the flower clusters a hairy or fringed appearance. The plant has been used medicinally as a purgative. Distribution of this species is chiefly mountainous and runs into western borders of the coastal plain at the northern and southern extremities. A second name for the plant is Culver's Physic. *Woods, meadows, streamsides.*

Lizard's Tail

× ¾

Saururus cernuus June–August

The stems of this plant run along the ground and send up branches to a height of 1½ to about 3 feet. The leaves are 2 to 5 inches long and heart-shaped. The very small flowers grow in a dense, slender cluster 4 to 8 inches long that characteristically droops at the tip. The flowers have no petals, and the white clusters owe their visibility to the color of the stamens and the flowering stalk. Another name for this plant is Water Dragon. *Swamps, marshes, wet woods, streamsides.*

Water Pennywort

× 1¼

Hydrocotyle verticillata   June–August

The slender stems lie on the ground and send up erect leaves
and flowering stalks. The leaves are nearly round with shallow
lobes, and the long stalks attach at the middle of the leaf
blade. The tiny white flowers are loosely clustered along the
length of a slender stalk. *H. umbellata* and *H. ranunculoides*
are similar species, but the former has flowers clustered only
at the tip of flowering stalk, and the latter has the leaves
cleft, so that the leaf stalk is attached to the edge of the
blade. *Wet woods, shallow water, wet pond and stream banks*

33

Man-of-the-earth

Ipomoea pandurata   June–September

The stems of this plant trail across the ground and sometimes
twine around other plants. The oval or heart-shaped leaves
are often narrow near the middle and are 1½ to 5 inches
long. The flowers are white with purple centers, grow in
clusters of 2 to 6, and are 2 to 3 inches long and broad. *I.
purpurea* is another somewhat similar morning glory, but the
flowers are usually blue or purple and without the different
colored "eye" in the center. Other species are cited in the
descriptions of *I. hederacea* and *I. coccinea*. The underground
parts of the plant are frequently greatly enlarged and are
edible. The American Indians are said to have eaten them.
Man-of-the-earth is also known as Man-root. *Roadsides, fields,
dry woods.*

34

White-topped Aster

Sericocarpus asteroides   × 1

Sericocarpus asteroides   June–September

This plant is 8 inches to 2 feet tall. The leaves are larger, stalked, and wider near the toothed tip on the lower part of the plant and smaller, stalkless, and often without teeth on the upper part. The flower heads have cream to brown flowers in the center and white on the border. All the flower heads together form a more or less flat-topped arrangement. A somewhat similar species, *S. linifolius*, is usually without basal leaves, and its upper leaves are smaller, narrow, and usually without teeth. *Dry woods and roadsides.*

35

Round-leaved Sundew

×1⅓

Drosera rotundifolia   June–September

This insectivorous plant grows upon or very close to the ground. The round leaves have slender stalks and sticky hairs that secrete dewlike drops. The white or pinkish flowers are on a smooth stalk 3 inches to about a foot long. *D. brevifolia* has hairy flower stalks and much shorter leaf stalks. *D. intermedia* and *D. capillaris* have leaves that are longer than wide, and the former has white flowers that may have a pink tint, while the latter has pink flowers. Stimulation of the leaf by a landing insect causes the hairs to bend toward the point of contact, and enzymes in the dewlike secretion digest the prey. Another fitting name for these plants is Daily Dew. *Bogs, swamps.*

Tread-softly

× ¾

Cnidoscolus stimulosus   June–September

The stems are 3 inches to over 2 feet tall and bear stinging hairs, as do practically all other parts of the plant. The leaves are long-stalked and are divided into 3 or 5 lobed and toothed segments. The white flowers, about an inch across, are clustered at the end of the stem. The effects of the stinging hairs seem to be more painful and long-lasting than those of some of the other species of stinging plants, and in some individuals the reaction is quite severe. Bull Nettle is another name for the plant. *Open, sandy woods and fields.*

37

Rose Mallow

Hibiscus moscheutos   June–September

The stems reach a height of 3 to 7 feet. The oval, toothed leaves taper to a point, sometimes have small lobes, and are 3 to 9 inches long and usually less than 4 inches wide. Flowers are 4 to 8 inches across and sometimes pink but always have a red center. *H. palustris* is very similar but usually has pink or sometimes white flowers without the red center and leaves usually 3-lobed and nearly as wide as long. *H. militaris* has dark reddish pink flowers with a red center and usually sharp-pointed lobes at the leaf bases. *H. syriacus* is a large shurb with purple, pink, or white flowers often planted and sometimes escaped. Another species *H. trionum*, and another similar species of the family, *Kosteletzkya virginica*, are described herein. Rose Mallow is also called Wild Cotton. *Marshes, wet meadows.*

38

Star Rush

×1¾

Dichromena colorata   June–September

The triangular stems are a foot to nearly 3 feet tall. The narrow leaves are grasslike. The very small flowers are enclosed in a series of white, flat, overlapping scales that develop in a dense cluster at the stem tip. The flowering cluster is surrounded by 4 to 7 leaves having white bases. Star Rush is also called White Top Sedge. *Open and wet areas, swamps, shallow water.*

39

Fragrant Water Lily

× ⅓

Nymphaea odorata June–September

The leaves of this aquatic plant float upon the surface of the water and are nearly round with a wedge-shaped opening on one side, 2 inches to about a foot across. The upper surface of the leaf is bright green and the lower usually purple or reddish. The fragrant flowers are white or rarely pink, 2 to 6 inches across, and composed of numerous petals. Flowers are more fully open during the morning hours. This species is also called Pond Lily. *Quiet water.*

Snow-on-the-mountain

× 1

Euphorbia marginata　　　　　　　　　　　　　　June–October

The hairy stems of this plant are a foot to 3 feet tall and contain milky juice. The oblong, stalkless leaves are 1½ to 4 inches long and usually in a circle just beneath the flowering branches. Many uppermost leaves are white-bordered or entirely white. Tiny white flowers are in a cuplike structure resembling a single flower. *E. corollata*, a common species, has dark green, oblong leaves often wider near the tip. Another species, *E. cyparissias*, is also cited. These plants are reported as poisonous. Snow-on-the-mountain is a native of the western United Stated introduced into the east as an ornamental and occasionally escapes from cultivation. *Roadsides, fields, streamsides.*

41

Gaura

Gaura biennis

× 1½

June–October

This hairy-stemmed plant grows to a height of 4 to 7 feet. The leaves are 2 to 5 inches long, narrowed at both ends, and margins usually have irregular teeth. The white flowers age to pink or red and are clustered at the ends of the stems. The petals are at the upper side of the flower rather than being more or less equally spaced in a circle. *Open woods, meadows, roadsides.*

42

Pokeberry

Phytolacca americana

× 1¾

June–October

The smooth green stems about 4 feet tall frequently become purple, as much as 3 or 4 inches in diameter, and nearly 10 feet tall late in the season. The large, smooth leaves are ½ to 1 foot long and taper gradually to a point. The flowers grow in elongate clusters opposite the leaves and are white, often tinged with green or pink. The fruits develop as hanging clusters of immature green or yellowish berries and mature purple-black ones. Despite the poisonous nature of the plant, especially the root, the young stems and leaves are cooked and eaten. Birds appear to become inebriated from eating the fermented fruits. Another common name used in Pigeonberry. *Roadsides, fields, pastures, moist woods.*

43

Rattlesnake Plantain

× ½

Goodyera pubescens   July–August

This orchid is 8 inches to 1½ feet tall and densely hairy. The leaves are clustered at the base of the stem and are 1½ to 4 inches long with whitish veins. The dense cluster of small white flowers may be 2½ to 3½ inches long. Another species, *G. repens*, is found in the mountains and is very similar except that the flowers may have a greenish or pink tint, and the flower cluster is usually one-sided. Another name for both these species is Lattice Leaf. *Dry or moist woods.*

Wintergreen

× 1¾

Gaultheria procumbens

July–August

This plant is 3 to 8 inches tall. The evergreen leaves are oval or almost round with toothed margins and a shiny surface. The flowers are usually white but occasionally have a pink tint. The fruit is a bright red berry that remains on the plant from winter until spring. Another species, *G. hispidula*, is more northerly, with leaves less than ½ inch long, white fruit, and a trailing habit. Wintergreen is an aromatic plant that is a source of oil of wintergreen. Another name for the species and its spicy fruits is Teaberry. *Dry or moist woods.*

Virgin's Bower

× ½

Clematis virginiana   July–September

This climbing vine often forms dense masses of tangled
stems. The leaves are divided into 3 segments that are
pointed, toothed, and often lobed, and each segment has a
conspicuous stalk. There are numerous large clusters of white
to cream flowers. During fruiting great quantities of silvery
plumes form that are nearly as striking as the floral display.
A similar species, *C. dioscoreifolia*, has leaves divided into 5
segments that are untoothed. Another species is cited in the
description of *C. crispa*. Virgin's Bower is also known as
Devil's Darning Needle. Repeated contact with its stem and
leaves has been reported to cause skin inflammation. *Moist
woods and roadsides, streamsides.*

Duck-potato

×½

Sagittaria latifolia   July–September

This aquatic plant may reach a height of nearly 4 feet. The variable leaves may be very slender and short or almost 1½ feet long and about as wide, usually with long, pointed lobes at the base giving the appearance of an arrowhead. The white flowers are about an inch to 1½ inches across. *S. engelmanniana*, much less common, is similar but has smaller leaves and flowers. *S. falcata* and *S. graminea* have slenderly oval leaves with long stalks, and the latter has many leaves barely an inch wide and somewhat grasslike. *S. subulata* is less than a foot tall and has leaves as much as 2 feet long but less than ½ inch wide. The underground stems were used as food by the Indians. *Ponds, streams, very wet soils.*

Turtlehead

Chelone glabra   July–September

This plant ranges from about 2 feet to almost 7 feet in height. The paired leaves are oval-pointed, 4 to 8 inches long, and vary in width from less than ¼ inch to over 2 inches. The flowers are basically white, but toward the tips they may be lightly or heavily tinted with pink, purple, or yellow. *C. obliqua* and *C. cuthbertii* are similar but less frequently occurring species; the former has entirely purple flowers, while the latter has leaf bases connected directly to the stem without a stalk. Snakehead is another name for these species. *Streamsides, wet woods, ditches, and pastures.*

Silverrod

$\times 1$

Solidago bicolor

July–October

The stems may be 6 inches to over 3 feet tall and are covered with whitish hairs. Leaves near the base of the stem are 2 to 8 inches long, toothed, usually wider near the tip, and narrowed to an abrupt point, and leaves are progressively smaller up the stem. The tiny white or yellowish flowers are in small clusters that resemble single flowers and make up a larger, elongate cluster. Some other species are cited in the descriptions of *S. juncea* and *S. caesia*. This species is also called White Goldenrod. *Open woods, roadsides, fields.*

49

Grass-of-Parnassus

× 1½

Parnassia asarifolia   August–October

This plant is found infrequently in the coastal plain and is chiefly a mountain species. The flowering stem is 6 inches to about 1½ feet tall. The leaves at the base of the flowering stem are heart-shaped to nearly round and long-stalked, while a single leaf about midway up the stem is stalkless. The flowers are about 1¼ inches across and are white with green streaks. Bog Star is another name for the plant. *Bogs, streamsides, wet woods.*

50

Shadow Witch

× 1⅓

Ponthieva racemosa　　　　　　　　　September–October

This rare orchid has a low cluster of basal leaves 1 inch to 6 inches long that taper abruptly to a point and are often wider near the tip. The flowers are white with greenish or yellowish veining. The flowering stalk is hairy and usually reddish brown but may be purplish brown or greenish brown. Shadow Witch is also called Ponthieu's Orchid. This orchid is at the northern limit of its range in southeastern Virginia. *Wooded pond margins and streamsides.*

51

Yellow Harlequin

× 1

Corydalis flavula   March–May

The plant is 5 inches to 1 ½ feet tall with spreading branches. The leaves are finely divided into many segments, and the lower leaves have long slender stalks. The flowers are entirely yellow and oriented at a right angle to the flower stalk. The fruit is a slender, pointed pod a little less than an inch long. This plant is more frequently distributed in the western half of the state. Another species, *C. sempervirens*, is chiefly mountainous but extends into the outer piedmont and has pink flowers with yellow tips. Yellow Harlequin is also known as Yellow Fumewort. *Rich woods, moist slopes, streamsides.*

Hispid Buttercup

Ranunculus hispidus   March—May

The hairy stems of this plant are 6 inches to 1½ feet tall.
The leaves are divided into 3 segments that are toothed and
lobed. The flowers have petals ½ to ¾ inch long, oblong,
and often a little wider at the tip. Each flower develops a
rounded cluster of flattened, disklike fruits. A species of
fields and roadsides, *R. bulbosus*, has a bulblike stem base.
Petals of *R. recurvatus*, of moist woods, are ¼ inch long or
less, while *R. sardous*, of fields and roadsides, has petals about
½ inch long. The 3 petals of *R. pusillus* are less than ⅛ inch
long, and the upper leaves are slender. The petals of *R.
abortivus* and *R. parviflorus* are ⅛ inch long or less; the basal
leaves of the former are toothed, while those of the latter are
toothed and lobed. Buttercups form a complex group requiring close examination of the fruits for identification. *Woods,
wood borders, meadows.*   53

Cinquefoil

Potentilla canadensis   March–May

The stems of this low-lying and spreading plant usually trail along the ground. The leaves are divided into 5 toothed segments. The flowers are about ½ inch across and scattered along the stem. *P. simplex* and *P. reptans* are both similar low-lying species, but the former has leaf segments toothed even to their bases, and the latter has 5 to 7 leaf segments and larger flowers. *P. norvegica*, *P. intermedia*, and *P. recta* are tall, erect plants; leaves of the first species are divided into 3 segments, the second into 5, and the third into 5 to 7 along with flowers twice as large and pale yellow. A second name for Cinquefoil is Five Finger. *Dry woods and fields, roadsides.*

Yellow Jessamine

× ¾

Gelsemium sempervirens   March–May

This species is an evergreen vine that may be climbing or trailing. The leaves are in pairs, 1½ to 3 inches long, and taper to a rounded or pointed tip. The flowers are about 1 inch long and fragrant. The fruit is an oblong, beaked pod that is somewhat flattened and about ½ inch long. Root extracts have been used as medicines, but most parts of the plant have been cited as poisonous. Evening Trumpet Flower is another name for this plant. *Woods, thickets, roadsides.*

Wild Pansy

$\times 1\frac{1}{4}$

Viola arvensis   March–June

The stems of this violet are 2 inches to about a foot tall. The leaves are oval to rounded at the tip with several narrow, fingerlike lobes at the base. The flowers are yellow with deeper yellow or yellowish orange within, and the upper part of the flower can be partly or entirely pale to dark purple. Another somewhat similar species is cited in the description of *V. kitaibeliana*. Wild Pansy, a native of Europe, is also known as European Field Pansy. *Roadsides, fields, wood borders.*

Cancer Root

×⅔

Conopholis americana   March–July

The stems are 2 to 10 inches tall, thick, tapered toward the tip, and scale-covered, giving the appearance of a pine cone. The small whitish flowers are partially covered by the scales. The entire plant is pale to dark brownish yellow. Cancer Root produces no chlorophyll and therefore no food. It is parasitic, as are all members of its family, upon the roots of trees, frequently oak. Squaw Root is another name for this plant. *Dry to moist woods.*

Spiny-leaved Sow Thistle × ½

Sonchus asper   March–July

This prickly plant ranges from a foot to over 6 feet in height.
The leaves are 2 to 12 inches long with spiny-toothed margins. Occasionally the leaf margins are lobed and toothed.
The base of the leaf has two rounded or curled lobes. The
very small flowers are arranged in a very dense cluster about
½ inch across. *S. oleraceus* is a very similar species but is
distinguished by its usually less prickly, more lobed leaf
margins and leaf bases that are much more pointed than
rounded. Both these species are European introductions that
have become a part of our flora. *Roadsides, fields, pastures.*

Indian Strawberry   × 1

Duchesnea indica   March–September

Leaves and flowers grow from a slender stem lying on the ground. The leaves are divided into 3 segments that are toothed and oval or tapered to a point. The flower is yellow and solitary at the end of a long stalk. The fruit is red, about ½ inch in diameter, and very similar to a small, cultivated strawberry, but it has little or no flavor. *Fragaria virginiana* and *F. vesca* both are very similar plants in general form and fruit shape and color, but both have white flowers and edible, sweet strawberries. The former has flowers nearly an inch across, and the latter has flowers about ½ that size. Indian Strawberry is known also as Snakeberry. *Moist woods and roadsides, lawns.*

Yellow Stargrass

Hypoxis hirsuta

× ¾

March–September

This plant is 2 inches to 2 feet tall. The leaves are narrow and long, superficially resembling grass leaves. There are usually 3 or more flowers on a stalk that is much shorter than the leaves. The flower color is pale to deep yellow, and the outer 3 flower parts are rounded at the tip. *H. micrantha* is a similar species with usually shorter leaves, 1 to 2 flowers on the stalk, and the outer three flower parts pointed. *H. sessilis* is a rare species with usually a solitary flower on a stalk often less than ½ inch long. *Open woods, meadows, roadsides.*

Merry Bells

×1

Uvularia sessilifolia   April–May

The slender stems are 4 inches to about a foot tall bearing leaves and flowers only in the upper part. The leaves are tapered at both ends and whitish beneath. The pale yellow flowers are about ½ to 1 inch long. *U. pudica* is a very similar plant but has shiny leaves without the whitish undercoat and usually grows in clumps. *U. perfoliata* has bright yellow flowers and leaves through which the stem appears to grow. A species of the mountains and central piedmont, *U. grandiflora*, may stand over 2 feet tall with flowers 2 inches long. Merry Bells is also called Wild Oats. *Rich woods, shaded slopes.*

61

Trumpets

$\times \frac{1}{3}$

Sarracenia flava   April–May

This insectivorous pitcher plant is a foot to over 3 feet tall. The leaves are tubular and hooded with a narrow wing extending along one side. The large yellow to greenish yellow flowers have bright yellow drooping petals that soon fall, as in the pictured specimen, before the "pitchers," within which insects are digested, attain their full height. Our only other species *S. purpurea*, has shorter bowed or "pot-bellied" pitchers and flowers with purple petals. Trumpets, also named Huntsman's-horn, reaches its northern limit in southeastern Virginia. *Bogs, wet roadside ditches.*

Marsh Marigold

× ⅓

Caltha palustris   April–June

Marsh Marigold has hollow stems that may be 8 inches to over 2 feet tall. The toothed leaves are 2 to 6 inches across, broadly heart-shaped to almost round. Most leaves are on the lower stem and have long stalks, while the upper leaves have shorter stalks or are stalkless. The flowers are about an inch to almost 2 inches across and bright yellow to orange-yellow with a cluster of stamens, or pollen-bearing organs in the center. *Marshes, swamps, wet meadows, shallow water.*

63

Meadow Parsnip

× ½

Thaspium barbinode   April–June

This plant is a foot to about 4 feet tall. Leaves are divided
into groups of 3 segments that are toothed and lobed with
very small bristly hairs at the base of the leaf stalk. Flower
clusters are composed of smaller groups of stalked, pale yellow flowers. *T. trifoliatum* is similar but has unlobed, small-
toothed leaf segments and some lower leaves heart-shaped.
Zizia aptera is very similar to *T. trifoliatum* but has a stalkless
center flower in each of the small clusters. *Z. trifoliata* and
Z. aurea have stalkless center flowers and all leaves 3-seg-
mented, but the former has larger, fewer teeth per segment,
while the latter has more, smaller teeth. *Dry or moist woods.*

Yellow Lady's Slipper

× ½

Cypripedium calceolus   April–June

This orchid is 8 inches to over 2½ feet tall. There are usually 3 to 5 leaves that are broad and 2 to 8 inches long. The flowers are about 2½ inches long, the upper and slender parts greenish yellow or purple and the lower, bulbous part pale to deep yellow with an opening. Another species is cited in the description of *C. acaule*. Yellow Lady's Slipper, also known as Golden Slipper, and others of the genus are reported to cause mild to severe skin inflammation upon handling. *Moist woods, swamps*.

Green and Gold

×1¼

Chrysogonum virginianum   April–June

The plant may appear to be stemless in early spring but later attains a height of almost 2 feet. The paired and long-stalked leaves are toothed, hairy, and 1 inch to 3½ inches long with the tips rounded or pointed. The compact cluster of very small flowers appears as a single yellow flower with 5 petals, since the flowers in the center of the cluster are all highly reduced, with only the 5 bordering flowers developing a large "petal." *Woods*.

66

Dwarf Dandelion   × 1

Krigia virginica   April–June

This plant is 2 to 15 inches tall and has slender, leafless stems with milky sap. The leaves are clustered at ground level and are ½ inch to about 4 inches long with pointed lobes that are often wider near the tip. The tiny yellow to orange-yellow flowers are clustered at the tip of the flower stalk. There are 2 species, *K. dandelion* and *Serinia oppositifolia*, that are similar, but the former has an enlarged underground stem, while the latter has leafy, and usually branched, stems. *Dry or sandy woods, roadsides, fields.*

Golden Club

× ⅓

Orontium aquaticum   April–June

This aquatic plant is about a foot to 2 feet tall. The thick-
stalked leaves arise in a cluster from the base of the plant and
are oval with the tips rounded or pointed. The curved flowering stalks are white toward the end where they bear a
cluster of bright yellow flowers. The lower portion of the
leaves and flowering stalks may be covered by water. *Shallow
water, wet pond or stream banks.*

Cypress Spurge

×1

Euphorbia cyparissias   April–July

The stems of this plant are 6 inches to about 2 feet tall and are usually found growing in dense tufts. There are numerous narrow, pale green leaves crowded on the stem. The very small flowers are yellowish green and lie between a pair of rounded or pointed, bright greenish yellow leaves that become orange, red, or purple with age. Other species are cited in the description of *E. heterophylla* and *E. marginata*. Although Cypress Spurge has been used medicinally, the milky juice is reported as poisonous. This species was introduced from Europe for ornamental planting and has escaped from cultivation into our flora. Another name is Cemetery or Graveyard Spurge. *Roadsides, fields, wood borders.*

69

Golden Ragwort

X ½

Senecio aureus   April–July

Stems are a foot to almost 4 feet tall. Lower leaves are larger, heart-shaped, toothed, and long-stalked. Clusters of small flowers resemble single flowers about an inch across with an orange-yellow center and yellow rays. *S. vulgaris* and *S. glabellus* have similar leaves throughout with the former's flower cluster lacking projecting rays and the latter's leaf lobes rounded. Remaining species have elongate, wide-tipped basal leaves. *S. pauperculus* and *S. obovatus* are similar, but the latter has more rounded leaf tips and stems running on the ground. *S. smallii* and *S. tomentosus* usually have 20 or more flower heads, and the latter has densely hairy lower stems and leaves and less deeply lobed leaves. Golden Ragwort, also Squaw Weed, is reported as poisonous. *Wet woods and meadows, swamps.*

Yellow Thistle

× 1

Cirsium horridulum April–July

The thick hairy stems of this plant are 8 inches to over 2½ feet tall. The leaves are 4 inches to about a foot long and divided into several lobed and sharply toothed segments. The large flower clusters are about 2 to 3 inches across and are encircled by several vertical and very spiny leaves. The flower color is pale to brownish yellow or occasionally purple. Some other species are cited in the description of *Carduus nutans*. *Roadsides, fields, meadows.*

Evening Primrose

× 1⅓

Oenothera laciniata   April–August

The spreading, hairy stems are 6 inches to over 2 feet tall.
The leaves are 1½ to 3 inches long and irregularly lobed.
Flowers are about an inch to 2 inches across and yellow to
red. The fruit is an elongate pod tapered to the tip. *O. biennis*
is similar but has unlobed leaves up to 6 inches long and
flowers 1½ to 2 inches across. *O. humifusa* is prostrate with
flowers less than an inch across and much smaller leaves. *O.
speciosa* has pink or white flowers 2 inches or more across. *O.
perennis* and *O. fruticosa* have fruits enlarged toward the tip,
and the former has flowers about an inch across and leaves to
2½ inches long and ½ inches wide, while the latter has
flowers about 2 inches across and leaves twice as large. *Fields,
roadsides.*

72

Low Hop Clover

× 1⅔

Trifolium procumbens   April–September

This clover has sprawling stems 2 inches to a foot tall. The leaves are divided into 3 segments, the middle segment having the longest stalk. The small yellow flowers are ½ inch long in clusters of about 20 to 40. *T. dubium* is very similar but with only 5 to 15 flowers in a cluster. *T. agrarium* is also a very similar species, but the leaf segments have stalks of about equal length or are stalkless. *T. repens* is the common white lawn clover, and the abundant clover with large clusters of pink flowers is *T. pratense*. The clover with bright red flowers is *T. incarnatum*. All of these clovers were introduced from Europe. Low Hop Clover is also called Hop Trefoil. *Roadsides, fields, lawns.*

Yellow Wood Sorrel

× 1¼

Oxalis stricta   April–October

The stems of this plant are 5 inches to a foot tall and frequently grow in dense clusters that form extensive mats. The leaves are divided into 3 segments that are heart-shaped. The flowers are about ½ to 1 inch across and occur in small clusters of usually less than 6 flowers. The fruits are pointed, hairy pods about ½ to 1 inch long, and the stalks project horizontally or downward from the stem. There are 2 somewhat similar species, *O. filipes* and *O. corniculata*, but the former has less hairy stems and fruits, and the latter has reclining stems rooted to the ground at several places. Another species is cited in the description of *O. rubra*. *Lawns, fields, open woods.*

Wild Radish

× 1⅓

Raphanus raphanistrum   April–October

This plant is a foot to over 2 feet tall with somewhat rough stems. The leaves are 3 to 8 inches long, rough, lobed, and usually broader near the tip. The flowers are about an inch across, and the petals are oval to almost round. The flower color varies from pale yellow to nearly white, and occasionally the veins are pinkish or bluish. The fruits are an inch to 2½ inches long, slender, and pointed. *R. sativus*, the cultivated radish, has pale pinkish purple flowers. The seeds of Wild Radish are said to be poisonous. Jointed Charlock is another name for this species. *Roadsides, fields.*

Indian Cucumber-root

× 1¾

Medeola virginiana   May–June

Stems are 8 inches to about 3 feet tall and usually hairy.
There is a circle of 5 to 10 leaves 2½ to 5 inches long about
midway up the stem and a circle of usually 3 smaller leaves
at the tip of the stem. The flowers are at the stem tip and are
yellow to greenish yellow with the inner parts, the stamens
and stigmas, reddish or brownish purple. The stigmas curve
back over the rest of the flower. There is a thickened underground stem, the "cucumber-root," that is edible. *Moist
woods.*

Lance-leaved Tickseed

Coreopsis lanceolata   May–July

The plant is 8 inches to over 3 feet tall. Leaves are chiefly basal, to 8 inches long, ½ to ¾ inch wide, usually unlobed, and wider near the top. Flower heads are an inch to 2½ inches across on stalks 4 to 15 inches long. *C. oniscicarpa* and *C. tripteris* have leaves ½ inch to 1½ inches wide, but those of the former are unlobed and highly reduced up the stem, while the latter's are 3-lobed. *C. auriculata* has unlobed or 3-lobed leaves that are broadly oval or round. Other species are cited in the description of *C. tinctoria*. Several members of this group of plants, known as tickseeds, coreopsis, and dye flowers, are cultivated as ornamentals. *Roadsides, dry woods, fields.*

King Devil

× ½

Hieracium pratense   May–July

This plant stands a foot to 3 feet tall. It is hairy, and the hairs on the upper stem are usually dark. The slender leaves at the base are 3 to 8 inches long, hairy, and rounded or pointed at the tip. The clusters of flowers at the end of the stem are covered basally with dark hairs. Two other similar species, *H. venosum* and *H. gronovii*, have wider leaves, and the former has purple-veined leaves, while the latter has a more narrow, elongate floral cluster. The name Hawkweed was given to these plants in reference to the belief that they were somehow responsible for the visual acuity of hawks. They are all European introductions. *Roadsides, fields, open woods.*

Ground Cherry

Physalis heterophylla

×1¼

May–August

The widely branching, hairy stems grow 6 inches to about 3 feet tall. The leaves are variable but usually are ovate, toothed, wider near the base or near the tip, and rounded to the base. The fruit resembles a Japanese lantern. *P. virginiana* and *P. pubescens* are similar, but the former has tapering leaf bases, while the densely hairy latter species has 5 anthers, or pollen-bearing organs, which are blue. *P. angulata* and *P. maritima* do not have the dark spots within the flower, and the former has blue anthers and the latter yellow. The leaves and immature fruits are said to be poisonous. *Woods, fields, roadsides.*

Cat's-ear

× ½

Hypochoeris radicata   May–August

There may be a single stem or several stems that are slender, usually branched, and appear leafless. Plants are 8 inches to about 2 feet tall. The leaves, except for very small ones, are all at the base of the plant, 2 to 6 inches long, coarse-haired, variously toothed and lobed, and frequently wider near the tip. The very small bright yellow flowers are in dense clusters at the ends of the stems and resemble single flowers nearly an inch across. *Pyrrhopappus carolinianus* is a somewhat similar species, but the leaves are smoother, usually narrower and pointed, and more evident on the upper stem; also, the tips of the small leaves surrounding the flower clusters resemble high-heeled shoes. *Roadsides, fields, lawns.*

Spatterdock

Nuphar advena   May–October

This aquatic plant has erect, well-developed leaves about as broad as they are long. If the plant is in water, the leaves emerge from the water. The flowers are cup-shaped to almost globular and yellow often tinged with green or red. *N. sagittifolium* has leaves 6 inches to 1½ feet long and only 2 to 5 inches wide, and both floating and submersed leaves are developed. Yellow Pond Lily is a name for both these species. *Ponds, pond margins, swamps, streams.*

Yellow Passion Flower

× 1¾

Passiflora lutea   June–August

This climbing vine has stems that may be 10 feet or more long and bear curling tendrils. The leaves have 3 shallowly cut lobes with the tips blunt or rounded and the margins smooth. The fringed flowers are about an inch across and yellow or greenish yellow. The fruit is round, about ½ inch in diameter, and purple or black. One other species, *P. incarnata*, has a purple or purplish pink fringe and is described herein. *Woods, wood borders.*

Fringed Loosestrife

Lysimachia ciliata   June–August

This plant is 6 inches to over 3 feet tall and usually well branched. The paired leaves are 2 to 6 inches long, oval-pointed, and have stalks ½ to 2 inches long lined with large hairs. The flowers are an inch or more across and have a single tooth at the tip of each petal. *L. lanceolata* has stalkless leaves that are usually very narrow and flowers ½ to ¾ inch across. *L. quadrifolia* has its leaves in circles and flowers with a reddish center and reddish or dark streaks on the petals. Another species is cited with *L. nummularia. Marshes, wet meadows, streamsides.*

83

Moneywort

× 1½

Lysimachia nummularia   June–August

The stems of this prostrate plant lie on the ground and become rooted at the sites where leaves are produced, frequently forming a thick, matted growth. The paired leaves are numerous and oval to nearly round. The flowers are about an inch across and yellow with very fine black specks. *L. radicans* usually has some reclining stems that take root, but the plant is usually m much more erect with leaves that taper gradually to a point and flowers ½ inch across. Other species are cited in the description of *L. ciliata*. Creeping Charlie is another name for Moneywort. *Streamsides, moist woods and roadsides.*

Fennel

Foeniculum vulgare   June–August

The large stems of this aromatic plant stand 3 to almost 7 feet tall. The leaves are divided into numerous needlelike segments so slender that the plant has the appearance of a green mist from a distance. The yellow flowers are in small clusters with the stalks arising from the same point, and these small clusters form a similar, much larger cluster 3 to 5 inches across. Fennel is a native of Europe that is cultivated for use in salads and as a flavoring. It has established itself in our flora. *Roadsides, fields, pastures.*

Flax

×1½

Linum medium   June–August

This plant is usually a foot to 2 feet tall with slender, straight stems. The leaves are numerous, less than an inch long, very narrow, and taper to a needlelike point. The yellow flowers are ½ to ¾ inch across on stiff, upswept branches. The fruit is less than ⅛ inch across and rounded with a flattened top. *L. floridanum* is very similar but has fruits oval and rounded on top. *L. striatum* has lower leaves in pairs and winged or angled stems. *L. virginianum* has usually a few lowest leaves paired and the fruit flattened on top. The source of linen and linseed oil, *L. usitatissimum*, has blue flowers and is an infrequent escape from cultivation. *Dry or moist and open soils, sandy roadsides.*

Flower-of-an-hour

× 1¼

Hibiscus trionum   June–September

The hairy stems are usually widely branching and 2 to 3 feet tall. The leaves are divided into 3 segments that are lobed or scalloped. The flowers are an inch to 2 inches across and are yellow with a dark reddish purple center and pale purplish bands along the petal margins. The flowers remain open only a short time during the day. The fruiting structures resemble Japanese lanterns. Some other species of the genus *Hibiscus* are cited in the description of *H. moscheutos*. Okra, *H. esculentus*, with large yellow flowers and elongate, cone-shaped pods, occasionally escapes from gardens, as does cotton, *Gossypium hirsutum*, another member of the family. *Roadsides, fields.*

Birdsfoot Trefoil

× 1¼

Lotus corniculatus   June–September

The stems of this species may stand erect or trail along the ground and are a foot to 2 feet long. The small leaves are about an inch long and are divided into 5 segments. The leaves are nearly stalkless, and the leaf segments are separated into two groups, one group of 2 segments at the stem and the other 3 segments at the tip. The flowers are ½ to ¾ inch long and are clustered at the end of long stalks. The flower color is yellow to orange. *L. americanus*, infrequent in the piedmont, has 3 segments and solitary pink flowers. Birdsfoot Trefoil, also called Bastard Indigo, came into this country from Europe. *Roadsides, fields*.

Spotted St. John's Wort

× ¾

Hypericum punctatum June–September

This plant is a foot to over 3 feet tall. The paired, oval leaves are an inch to 2½ inches long, ½ inch wide, and covered with black dots. The yellow flowers are about ½ inch across and also black-dotted. *H. perforatum* is also black-dotted but has 4-angled or winged stems. *H. gentianoides* has leaves and flowers ⅛ inch long. *H. setosum* and *H. denticulatum* have flowers ½ inch across and leaves about ½ inch long, but the latter has 4-angled stems, *H. canadense* has flowers ¼ inch across and leaves ⅛ inch wide, *H. gymnanthum* and *H. mutilum* have flowers less than ⅛ inch wide and leaves ¼ to ¾ inch wide, but the former has triangular leaves. *Roadsides, fields, open woods.*

89

Water Stargrass

× 1¾

Heteranthera dubia   June–September

This rare species has its stems submerged in shallow water or in very wet mud. The leaves are very narrow and 2 to 6 inches long. The flowers are slender, an inch to 2½ inches long, and about ½ inch across. Water Stargrass, although far different in general appearance, is a member of the same family as the familiar Pickerelweed and is present only in the extreme northern tip of the coastal plain–fall zone region. Mud Plantain is another name for this plant, but this name certainly does not fit the picture of the flowers of this species upon a stream surface. *Shallow water or very wet banks.*

Pencil Flower

× 1¾

Stylosanthes biflora   June–September

The stiff stems of this plant are 4 inches to over 1½ feet tall. The leaves are divided into 3 segments that are ½ to 1½ inches long and oblong with a small, sharp projection at the tip. The leaf bases, just beneath the flowers, are bristly. The flowers are pale yellow to deep orange-yellow, often with reddish markings. *S. riparia* is a very similar species that usually has a spreading or straggling habit, and the bases of the uppermost leaves are not bristly. *Roadsides, fields*.

Sneezeweed

× ¾

Helenium nudiflorum   June–September

The winged stems are a foot to 3 feet or more tall. The leaves near the ground are oblong, often wider near the tip, and 3 to 7 inches long, while the upper leaves are an inch to 2 inches long and narrow. Flower heads consist of many small brown or purplish brown flowers and yellow bordering flowers. *H. brevifolium* is a more infrequent species with basal leaves an inch to 3 inches long and usually only about 1 to 4 flower heads. *H. autumnale* is usually without basal leaves at flowering time, and the upper leaves are 2½ to 6 inches long and ½ inch to over an inch wide. The central flowers of this latter species are yellow. Another species, *H. tenuifolium*, is described herein. *Moist roadsides and fields.*

Partridge Pea

× 1

Cassia fasciculata   June–September

This plant is 6 inches to 2 feet tall. Leaves are divided into
narrow segments about ½ inch long. The yellow flowers are
often purple at the center and are about an inch to 1 ½ inches
across. The fruit is a flattened pod an inch to 3 inches long.
C. nicitians has flowers about ½ inch or less across with very
unequal petals. These species have leaf segments more than
an inch long. *C. tora* has 2 to 3 pairs of widely rounded
segments. *C. occidentalis* has segments that are slenderly
pointed, and *C. marilandica* has 4 to 8 pairs of segments with
blunt-pointed or rounded tips. Several members of this genus
have a history of medicinal use. The name Golden Cassia is
also used for Partridge Pea. *Roadsides, fields, open woods, sandy
soils.*

Three-lobed Coneflower

× ½

Rudbeckia triloba

June–October

This thickly branched plant grows 1½ to 6 feet tall. The leaves are generally ovate to almost heart-shaped with some 3-lobed. The flowers are very small and of two colors. Dark purple central flowers and yellow to orange bordering flowers make up a densely packed cluster. *R. laciniata* flower clusters are greenish yellow in the center. *R. fulgida*, *R. hirta*, and *R. heliopsidis* have no lobed leaves, and the first two species have stalkless upper leaves. The leaves and green bases of the flower clusters of *R. hirta* are densely hairy, while *R. heliopsidis* has stalked leaves. *Woods, fields, roadsides.*

Goldenrod

× ½

Solidago juncea   June–October

The plant is a foot to over 4 feet tall. Leaves at the base are 6 inches to over a foot long, long-stalked, toothed, and wider near the tip, but they become stalkless, narrow, and nearly toothless up the stem. Often there are tufts of small leaves at the base of some of the upper leaves. The flowering area is frequently 6 inches to a foot across with down-curving branches having flowers only on the upper sides. *S. pinetorum* is a very similar species but has smaller leaves. Other species are cited with *S. bicolor* and *S. caesia*. Though often blamed as the culprit, the large group of many very similar plants called Goldenrod does not cause "hay fever." *Roadsides, fields, open woods.*

95

Bitterweed

Helenium tenuifolium   June–November

This plant is 6 inches to over 2 feet tall with thickly branching stems. The leaves are about an inch to 3 inches long, only about ⅛ inch wide, and very crowded on the stems. The flowering heads are usually numerous and about an inch across. The central flowers are a dull yellow, and the bordering flowers are brighter yellow. Other species are cited in the description of *H. nudiflorum*. Bitterweed contains a toxic principle, and a bitterness is passed on to the milk of cows grazing on the plant. This species is one member of a group called Sneezeweed. *Roadsides, fields, pastures.*

Sea Oats

Uniola paniculata

× ½

June–November

Sea Oats stand 3 to 6 feet tall. The narrow leaves are 8 inches to 2 feet long and taper to a slender point. The tiny flowers are enclosed in an overlapping series of flat, pointed, scalelike structers crowded into a dense cluster at stem ends. The flower cluster is pale to dark yellow or brownish yellow. *U. latifolia* has shorter, wider leaves without the slender-pointed tips and loose, drooping flower clusters. *U. laxa* and *U. sessiliflora* have much narrower flowering clusters, and the latter has clusters bearing few or no branches. Sea Oats not only enhance the picturesqueness of the sea beaches but are important natural elements of dune stabilization. *Dunes, coastal sands.*

Horse Balm

Collinsonia canadensis

×2

July–September

This plant has freely branching stems 1½ to nearly 5 feet tall. The large leaves are in pairs, 2 to 8 inches long, 2 to 7 inches wide, toothed, and pointed. The largest leaves on the lower stem have long stalks, while uppermost leaves are frequently stalkless. The flowers are only about ½ inch long but are numerous, and often the flowering portion of the plant may be 6 inches to a foot long. The plant has the odor of lemon, and oils extracted from it have been used medicinally. Richweed is another name for this species. *Moist woods, streamsides.*

False Foxglove

Gerardia pedicularia

× 1¼

August–September

The freely branching stems are 1½ to about 3 feet tall and hairy, with many of the hairs having enlarged tips. Most of the leaves are an inch to 2½ inches long with many lobes and teeth. The flowers are about 1½ inches across on stalks about ½ to 1 inch long. Two other species, *G. virginica* and *G. flava*, are somewhat similar, but their leaves are larger and much less lobed, and the former has flowers stalkless or nearly so, while the latter has stems without hairs and grows to a height of about 8 feet. These plants are parasitic upon the roots of oaks. *Dry woods, wood borders, clearings.*

Wreath Goldenrod

× 1

Solidago caesia   September–October

The often arching stems of this plant are a foot to over 3 feet tall and usually have a bluish coating that rubs off. Leaves are 2 to 5 inches long, about ½ to an inch wide, toothed, and stalkless. The yellow flower heads are clustered in the leaves near the ends of the stem. *S. curtisii* is a very similar species without the bluish stem coat and with leaves that are a little longer and wider, but it is a plant of the mountains. Wreath Goldenrod is also called Blue-stem Goldenrod. *Moist woods, wood borders, streamsides.*

Modiola

×2

Modiola caroliniana   April–June

This infrequent, low-growing plant has hairy stems that are erect or lying on the ground. The leaves are often nearly round in outline and deeply lobed and toothed. The flowers are less than ½ inch across and reddish orange, yellowish orange, or purplish orange with a dark purple center. The fruits are round, flat, and divided into narrow segments that give the overall appearance of a sliced pie. *Malva neglecta* is somewhat similar but has white, pale pink, or pale purplish blue flowers and much more shallowly lobed leaves. *Lawns, roadsides, fields.*

101

Candyweed

× ½

Polygala lutea   May–October

Stems are frequently clustered and stand 6 inches to about
1½ feet tall. Lower leaves are an inch to 2 inches long,
oblong, and often wider at the tip, while upper leaves are
reduced. The flowers are bright orange to yellowish orange
in dense, cylindrical clusters at the ends of the stems. *P.
ramosa* has a highly branched, broad cluster of light yellow
flowers. *P. curtissii* has purple flowers tipped with yellow, and
P. mariana is similar but without the yellow tips. *P. polygama*
has many leafy stems, leaves ½ inch long and ¼ inch wide,
and pink to purple flowers loosely arranged in slender clusters
2 to 8 inches long. Other species are cited in the description
of *P. cruciata*. Candyweed also bears the name Yellow Milkwort. *Bogs, swamps, wet open woods.*

Blackberry Lily

× ½

Belamcanda chinensis   June–July

This plant grows from about a foot to over 3 feet tall. The long swordlike leaves are progressively smaller up the plant, and the leaf bases clasp the stem. The flowers are arranged in a branching cluster with usually 1 or 2 open flowers and several buds. When the fruit matures and opens, there is a small mass of black seeds left in the center of the flower. This Asian species has escaped cultivation into our flora. *Roadsides, fields.*

Butterfly Weed

Asclepias tuberosa   June–August

The hairy stems of this plant grow at an angle and are a foot to over 2 feet tall. The numerous hairy leaves are alternate on the stem, narrow, and 1½ to 4 inches long. The flowers are usually a bright orange, but the color may vary from yellow to red. The fruits are slender pods 3 to 6 inches long and ½ inch in diameter. *A. incarnata* is 2 to 5 feet tall with pink to red flowers. Another species, *A. lanceolata*, has flower color very similar to Butterfly Weed and is described herein. Pleurisy Root is another name for Butterfly Weed, in reference to the belief that the underground parts of the plant contain some substance that will cure pleurisy. *Roadsides, fields.*

Orange Touch-me-not

× 1½

Impatiens capensis   June–September

This plant is 2 to 5 feet tall and is usually freely branched. The leaves are 2 to 5 inches long, an inch to 3 inches wide, and toothed. The orange, spurred flowers are usually spotted with reddish brown. The fruits are capsules about ¾ inch long. *I. pallida*, a more inland species, is very similar but has yellow flowers. The ripened fruits burst when touched, scattering the seeds in every direction. Rubbing the squashed leaves on areas of the skin that have been in contact with Poison Ivy appears to lessen the toxic effects. Another name for this plant is Jewelweed. *Moist woods, marshes, streamsides.*

Turk's-cap Lily

Lilium superbum   July–August

This large, many-flowered lily may be 10 feet or more tall. The leaves are 4 to 7 inches long and grow in circles of 6 to 15 along the stem. The flowers are yellowish orange to reddish orange and spotted within the strongly back-curved segments. There are commonly 5 to 15 flowers and sometimes as many as 50 or more. *L. michauxii* and *L. tigrinum* both have orange, spotted flowers with the parts curved back, but the former has far fewer flowers and leaves broader near the tip, while the latter, a cultivated species, has numerous single leaves bearing small black bulbs and is usually found near garden sites. *Wet woods and meadows, low roadsides.*

Yellow Fringed Orchid

×1

Habenaria ciliaris   July–August

The height of this orchid may be 1 foot to more than 3 feet.
The leaves toward the base of the plant are 3 to 12 inches
long; the upper leaves are smaller. The flowers are about ½
inch long and bright orange to yellow-orange. The flower
cluster is 2 to 6 inches long and 1½ to 3 inches thick. *H.
cristata* is a similar species but has smaller flowers and usually
a longer, more slender flower cluster. *H. blephariglottis* is also
similar but has white flowers. Yellow Fringed Orchid also has
the name Orange Plume. *Bogs, wet woods, thickets, streamsides.*

Cotton Grass

×1¾

Eriophorum virginicum   July–September

This infrequent sedge may be 2 to 4 feet tall. The very narrow leaves are 1 foot to 3 feet long and triangular at the tips. The tiny flowers are enclosed in a small, dense cluster of flat scales at the stem tip. The conspicuous feature of the flowering portion of the plant is the very dense plume of soft, pale brown bristles that become reddish brown or orange through the season. There is a similarity to a small boll of cotton, and the color of the bristles has given a second name, Tawny Cotton Grass, to the plant. *Bogs.*

Wild Columbine

×1

Aquilegia canadensis   April–June

The plant is a foot to 3 feet tall and is more often found in the mountains. The leaves are divided into groups of 3 segments that are toothed or lobed. The flower color is basically bright red with some yellow but can be varying shades of pinkish red. A cultivated species, *A. vulgaris*, sometimes escapes into the wild and is similar in form, but the flowers are blue or blue and white. Wild Columbine has been called Honeysuckle along with several other dissimilar species. *Moist to dry rocky woods and ledges.*

Drummond Phlox

× ½

Phlox drummondii April–July

The hairy stems are 6 inches to over 2 feet tall. The leaves are paired except near the stem tip. The flowers are red, purple, or white, or variable combinations of these colors. *P. paniculata* has leaves about an inch to 1½ inches wide with conspicuous veins. *P. glaberrima* has leaves only about ½ inch wide, and *P. maculata* has stems usually spotted or streaked with red and elongate, cylindrical flower clusters. Other species are cited in the description of *P. subulata*. Drummond Phlox also bears the name Annual Phlox and is a Texas native that has been introduced in the east by way of escape from cultivation. *Roadsides, fields, wood borders.*

Cross Vine

× 1

Bignonia capreolata   May

This vine may climb to a height of about 50 feet. The leaves
are in pairs and divided into 2 oblong segments 2 to 6 inches
long and a curling tendril. The flowers are about 2 inches
long and vary in color from red to orange-red outside and
yellow to orange-yellow inside. The fruit is a flattened pod 6
to 8 inches long, pointed at both ends, and containing
winged seeds about an inch to 1 ½ inches long. The bicolored
flowers and deep green leaves that change to the color of
copper or bronze mark this species as one of unusual beauty.
Moist woods, low streamsides.

111

Poppy

× ¾

Papaver dubium   May–June

The hairy stems are about a foot to 2 feet tall. The leaves are hairy, an inch to 4 inches long, and divided into many lobes that are toothed. The flowers are red and about 1½ to 2 inches across. The fruits are oval-shaped. *P. rhoeas* and *P. somniferum* escape infrequently from cultivation; the former has purplish red or white flowers with a dark center, while the latter has toothed leaves that clasp the stem. This last species is the source of the seeds used in baking and is also the source of opium. *Roadsides, fields.*

Hoary Pea

× 1

Tephrosia spicata   May–August

The stems are hairy and trail along the ground, usually be-
coming erect toward the tip. The leaves are divided into
several oblong segments each with a very slender, pointed
bristle at the tip. The flowers are about ¾ inch long and at
first are white but turn pink and then deep red or purplish
red. The fruits are hairy pods about 1½ inches long. Another
species, *T. virginiana*, is an erect plant with a dense cluster of
pink and yellow flowers at the ends of the stems. *Roadsides,
open woods, fields.*

Ginseng

×½

Panax quinquefolius   June–July

This is chiefly a plant of the mountains, but it is not plentiful anywhere. It is 8 inches to about 2 feet tall. There are usually 3 or 4 leaves, and each leaf is divided into 5 segments that are 2 to 6 inches long and toothed. The flowers are very small and white or greenish white. The fruits are bright red berries. The dried underground parts of this plant are highly valued in Chinese medicine, and populations have been markedly depleted by overcollecting for sale purposes. Ginseng is also known as Sang. *Rich woods.*

114

Mullein Pink

×¾

Lychnis coronaria   June–August

This plant is a foot to nearly 3 feet tall and covered with gray or white hairs. The leaves are in pairs, stalkless, pointed, and often wider near the tip. The flowers are deep purplish red, about ½ inch across, and solitary at the end of a long stalk. Another species with white flowers, *L. alba*, is included here. This plant is a native of Europe that was introduced for ornamental purposes and has escaped cultivation into our flora. *Roadsides, wood borders.*

Red Milkweed

× 1¼

Asclepias lanceolata   June–August

This milkweed stands 3½ to about 4 feet tall. The paired leaves are 3 to 8 inches long, narrow, tapered at both ends, and widely spaced on the stem. The flowers are bright orange-red to yellowish orange. Another species of milkweed, *A. tuberosa*, has similarly colored flowers and is described herein. Many species of the genus *Asclepias* are poisonous. *Wet pine woods and grassy areas, swamps, brackish marshes.*

Calliopsis

Coreopsis tinctoria   June–August

The stems stand a foot to about 4 feet tall with many branches. The leaves are divided into several very slender segments. The tiny flowers form a cluster resembling a single flower with a red or purple center and a red, yellow, or red and yellow border. Two other species, *C. grandiflora* and *C. verticillata*, also have very slender leaf segments, but the former has the "flower" toothed on the margin, while the latter has smooth or very inconspicuously toothed margins. Other species are cited in the description of *C. lanceolata*. Calliopsis, also called Golden Coreopsis and Tickseed, is a native of western United States that has escaped from its widespread planting as an ornamental. *Roadsides, fields, meadows.*

117

Corn Cockle

× ¾

Agrostemma githago   June–September

This plant is 1 foot to 3 feet tall and has slender stems. The narrow, pointed leaves are 2 to 5 inches long and grow in pairs. The red petals of the flowers have black spots at the bases. At the base of the flower are 5 slender green lobes that project beyond the petals, making a distinctive identifying feature. The fruit is oval and almost an inch long with the 5 lobes at the tip. The plant is a European introduction that, due to its natural habitat, may be harvested along with cereal grains, causing a troublesome situation in that the seeds are poisonous. Purple Cockle is another name of this species. *Grain fields, roadsides.*

Pinesap

Monotropa hypopithys   May–October

Pinesap grows to a height of from 3 inches to over a foot tall. The small leaves are scalelike. The plant may be yellow, reddish brown, pink, red, or some combination of these colors. Early in the season the color is predominantly yellow, while later on there are more pink and red plants. Unlike most flowering plants, it produces no chlorophyll, and it obtains food from other plants. The number of flowers may vary from 2 or 3 to 20 or more. The plants usually grow in clusters quite variable in size and number. *M. uniflora* is usually white with a single larger flower. *Monotropsis odorata* is a similar, smaller plant with the petals fused together. Pinesap is known also by the name False Beech-drops. *Litter of moist or dry woods.*

119

Cardinal Flower

Lobelia cardinalis   July–September

The usually unbranched stem of this plant attains a height of 2 to 7 feet. The toothed leaves are 2 to 8 inches long and taper to a point or rounded tip. The cluster of intensely red flowers can be 4 to almost 20 inches long. The stamens near the central part of the flower appear as points of gleaming white. There are 3 species with blue flowers ½ inch long or less. *L. nuttallii* is very slender with white-centered flowers having 2 green spots. *L. inflata* has flowers with the lower part much enlarged as fruiting begins, and *L. spicata* has dense clusters of very pale blue or white flowers. Other species are cited in the description of *L. siphilitica*. The color and size of the flower clusters of Cardinal Flower make it one of the most striking species of wildflowers. *Marshes, streamsides, wet woods and meadows.*

120

Wild Poinsettia

Euphorbia heterophylla × 1½

July–September

This poinsettia is usually characterized by low growth but may be about 3 feet tall. The leaves are variable on the same plant but some usually have a fiddle shape, and some upper leaves are partly or entirely red or white. The tiny yellowish flowers are hardly recognizable as such and are clustered in small cuplike structures that resemble the base of a single flower. Fruits are 3-lobed pods about ½ inch in diameter. *E. dentata* is a similar species with variable leaves, but more leaves are slender, tapered to a point, and toothed. Other species are cited with the descriptions of *E. marginata* and *E. cyparissias*. The poinsettia of commerce is *E. pulcherrima*. Wild Poinsettia is also called Painted Leaf. *Roadsides, fields, lawns.*

121

Red Morning Glory

× 1¼

Ipomoea coccinea   August–October

The slender, smooth stems grow by twining to a height of 2 to 10 feet. The leaves are heart-shaped, sometimes toothed, and often have angular lobes. The red flowers are an inch or more long and ½ to ¾ inch across. *I. quamoclit* has red flowers averaging a little larger and leaves that are divided into very slender segments. Both of these species are native to tropical America and have escaped from cultivation. Other species are cited with the descriptions of *I. pandurata* and *I. hederacea.* These plants are known also by the name Cypress Vine. *Roadsides, fields, fencerows, thickets.*

122

Trailing Arbutus

Epigaea repens   February–April

This low evergreen shrub has stems that lie on the ground.
The rough, hairy leaves are oblong to almost round and 1
inch to 4 inches long. The flowers grow in clusters at the
ends of the stems. The flowers are fragrant and may be pale
to deep pink or white. The creeping stems sometimes form
dense mats with the flowers partially hidden by the leaves.
Trailing Arbutus is also known as Mayflower. *Sandy or rocky
woods.*

Spring Beauty

× 1¼

Claytonia virginica   March–May

The stems of Spring Beauty are 2 inches to approximately a foot tall. There is a single pair of slender leaves about midway up the stem 2 to 8 inches long, less than ½ inch wide, and tapered at both ends with little or no stalk. The flowers are about an inch across and vary from a very pale pink to deep pink with reddish pink streaks within. There is one other similar species in the mountains, *C. caroliniana*, that has leaves that are wider, round-tipped, and stalked. The bright pink flowers make this plant a favorite of the early spring flora. *Moist woods, clearings, wood borders.*

Red Wood Sorrel

Oxalis rubra

× 1¼

March–September

This plant grows from 3 to 8 inches tall. The leaves are divided into 3 segments that are heart-shaped, and the hairy leaf stalks arise directly from the ground. The flowers are deep pink or once in a while white, and the flower stalks and lower green portion of the flowers are hairy. The species *O. violacea* is very similar, but the leaf and flower stalks and lower flower parts are smooth rather than hairy. Other yellow-flowered species are described in the treatment of *O. stricta*. The sour taste of the plant comes from a substance that is poisonous in large quantities; yet leaves of some species are salad items. This is a Brazilian introduction that has escaped cultivation. *Lawns, fields, roadsides.*

Moss Pink

×1

Phlox subulata   April–May

This phlox grows in low, sometimes extensive, mats. The leaves are short, pointed, slender and arranged in pairs or clusters. The flowers are about ¾ inch across and pale to deep pink, purple, or white, often with a darker center. A very similar species, *P. nivalis*, usually has less deeply notched petals or sometimes petals without a notch. *P. divaricata* has notched blue petals and usually 4 pairs of short, narrow leaves. Other species are cited in the description of *P. drummondii*. Moss Pink, also called Rock Pink, comes into the western border counties of the coastal plain but escapes limitedly from cultivation elsewhere. *Roadsides, sandy or rocky soils.*

126

Pinxter-flower

× 1

Rhododendron nudiflorum   April–May

This is a shrub 2 to 7 feet tall. The leaves develop after the flowers and are 2 to 4 inches long, pointed at both ends, often wider nearer the tip, and short-stalked. The flowers are very pale pink to deep pink, odorless or faintly fragrant, and the tubular portion of the flower is about as long as the flared petal lobes. The fruits are oblong, ½ inch to nearly an inch long, covered with stiff hairs, and persist into the winter. A very similar species is *R. canescens*, but the floral tube is longer than the petal lobes. A smaller plant, *R. atlanticum*, is only about a foot to 1 ½ feet tall and has white or purplish flowers. A later flowering species, *R. viscosum*, has white flowers from June to August. Pinxter-flower is also called Wild Azalea, and it is one of the early spring standouts, adding its numerous pink flowers to the landscape. *Dry or moist woods, swamps.*

Robin's Plantain

× 1

Erigeron pulchellus   April–May

The hairy, hollow stems are 4 inches to 2 feet tall. The leaves near the stem base are wider near the tip, toothed, and an inch to 7 inches long. Leaves are progressively smaller up the stem and clasp the stem. The flower heads are an inch or more across and usually in clusters of 2 to 5. Flower color varies from blue or pinkish blue to white. *E. philadelphicus* is similar but has stem leaves with earlike lobes at the base. *E. bonariensis* and *E. canadensis* have very small flower heads, and those of the former are densely hairy at the base. Other species are cited in the description of *E. strigosus*. *Open woods, meadows, roadsides.*

Swamp Pink

× ¼

Helonias bullata   April–May

This is a rare species that has evergreen leaves, long flower stalks, and dense flower clusters. The leaves are 4 inches to a foot long, usually wider near the tip, and form thick mats on the ground. The bright pink flowers are arranged in thick clusters an inch to about 4 inches long and an inch or more thick. This plant is not abundant anywhere and comes into only one county at the western border of the coastal plain. *Bogs, swamps.*

129

Wild Pink

Silene caroliniana   April–June

This is a plant that grows in tufts 2 to 10 inches tall. The paired leaves are 2 to 5 inches long, blunt or tapered to a short point, and usually wider near the tip. The white to very deep pink flowers are an inch or more across with petals sometimes notched. *S. noctiflora* has white, pink-tinged flowers that open in the evening, deeply cleft petals, and hairy, sticky stems. *S. antirrhina* has much smaller flowers and stems with dark sticky patches about midway between the leaves. *S. stellata* has flowers with fringed petals and leaves in circles. Another species, *S. cucubalus*, is included here. The sticky-stemmed species are known as Catchfly. *Sandy or rocky woods or wood borders.*

Showy Orchis

×1

Orchis spectabilis   April–June

This orchid is 3 inches to over a foot tall. There are usually 2 broad, rounded leaves clasping the flowering stalk at ground level. The thick flowering stalk bears several flowers with a small leaf below each one. The upper parts of the flower are pink, blue-pink, or purple, and the lower part is white. Flowers are about an inch long and ½ inch wide. The plant may form fairly extensive colonies. *Rich woods.*

131

Dovesfoot Cranesbill

× 1⅔

Geranium molle   April–July

This geranium is 4 inches to almost 2 feet tall with spreading, hairy stems. The soft, hairy leaves are broadly heart-
shaped to round and divided into 3 lobes, in turn lobed. The
pink or reddish pink flowers are about ½ inch across and
have deeply notched petals. Fruits are slender, pointed cones
about ½ inch long. *G. pusillum* is very similar but is less
hairy and has pale pink flowers with shallowly notched petals.
The lower green segments of the flowers of *G. carolinianum*
and *G. dissectum* have spiny tips, and the pale pink flowers of
the former are about an inch across, in contrast to the purple-
pink ½-inch flowers of the latter. *G. maculatum* has purple or
pinkish purple flowers usually an inch to nearly 2 inches
across and a pair of leaves about 2 inches across below the
flowers. *Lawns, roadsides, fields.*

Pink Lady's Slipper

Cypripedium acaule   April–July

This orchid is 6 inches to almost 2 feet tall. There are 2 leaves at ground level that are broad and 4 to 8 inches long. The flower may be 1 ½ to nearly 3 inches long. The upper, slender parts of the flower are yellowish green to greenish or purplish brown, and the lower, bulbous part is deep pink with reddish veining and cleft down the middle. Two other orchids are called Lady's Slipper. *C. calceolus* has yellow flowers, and *C. reginae*, which is rare and is found in the northern, mountainous part of the state, has pink and white or all white flowers. Handling of these orchids has been known to result in mild to severe skin inflammation. Pink Lady's Slipper also goes by the name Pink Moccasin Flower. *Moist to dry woods, swamps.*   133

Field Madder

× 1¼

Sherardia arvensis   April–August

This infrequent, freely branching plant often forms dense mats and is 4 inches to nearly 2 feet tall with square, hairy stems. The small leaves are about ½ inch long, pointed, and hairy and grow in circles of 4 to 6. The diminutive flowers are no more than ⅙ inch long and cluster in a bowl-shaped fusion of very small leaves. The flower color varies from pink to bluish pink or blue. There are several species of *Galium* with small flowers and leaves in circles, but the flowers are usually white, yellowish white, or greenish white and not enclosed in the bowl-shaped heads. *Roadsides, fields, lawns.*

134

Fumitory

× 1⅔

Fumaria officinalis   April–August

This infrequent plant has loosely spreading stems with many branches and leaves. The leaves are divided into many narrow segments. The small flowers are less than ½ inch long and pink or purplish pink with a dark red or purplish red tip. Fumitory was once thought to have great value as a medicine. The name Earth Smoke has been applied in reference to the odor of the fresh roots. The plant is a European species. *Roadsides, fields.*

Wild Onion

Allium canadense   May–June

This plant is slender and 8 inches to 2 feet tall. The leaves are about 4 inches to a foot long and less than ½ inch wide. The flowers are pink or white, about ½ inch across, and clustered with several bulblike structures at the end of the stem. All parts of the plant have the odor of onion. Another species, *A. vineale*, is very similar but has tubular leaves and often clusters of the bulblike structures with twisted stalks instead of flowers. Yet another, *A. cernuum*, has a crook in the stem, so that the flower cluster nods. The species *A. ampelo-prasum* is included here. Wild Onion is also called Wild Garlic. *Open woods, roadsides, fields.*

Rose Pogonia

Pogonia ophioglossoides   May–July

The height of this infrequent orchid varies from 4 inches to over 2 feet. There is usually a single leaf an inch to 4 inches long about midway up the stem and another smaller leaf just beneath the flower, but sometimes a leaf or two arise from the base of the stem. Generally a lone flower develops, but occasionally 2 or 3 flowers are present. Flower color is usually deep pink but can grade to a very pale pink. A rare species, *Arethusa bulbosa*, is somewhat similar, but only a single leaf develops that is much narrower, at the time when the fruit is maturing. Rose Pogonia is also known as Snake-mouth. *Bogs, wet meadows, pond margins with peat.*

Rabbit Foot Clover

× 1¼

Trifolium arvense   May–September

This clover is 4 inches to about 1 ½ feet tall with numerous branches and softly hairy throughout. The leaves are divided into 3 narrow segments about ½ to 1 inch long and wider near the tip. The very small pink-petaled flowers are in compact clusters and hidden by the dense, soft hairs, the "rabbit foot." Often the pink color is seen only at the tip of the cluster. Several other species of clover are cited in the description of *T. procumbens*. Rabbit Foot Clover, also called Old Field Clover, is reported as hazardous to grazing animals. *Fields, roadsides.*

Cranberry

× 1¾

Vaccinium macrocarpon

June–July

The stems of this evergreen plant trail along the ground, branch frequently, and form a matted growth. The leaves are oblong and round-tipped, dark green, and about ¼ to ¾ inch long. The flowers are pale pink to nearly white. The fruits are red berries about ½ inch in diameter, and they remain on the plant through the winter. This plant is the one widely cultivated for commercial purposes. It is also called Large or American Cranberry. *Bogs, pond margins with peat moss.*

139

Meadow Beauty

$\times$ 1

Rhexia virginica   June–September

The stems grow 7 inches to over 3 feet tall and are 4-winged. The leaves are 1 inch to nearly 3 inches long, paired, toothed, and more or less pointed at both ends. The flower color is usually purplish pink but varies from pale pink to reddish purple. The fruit is urn-shaped and about ½ inch long. *R. mariana* and *R. ciliosa* are similar, but the former has no wings on the stem, and the latter has very narrow wings and shorter, more ovoid leaves. *Wet meadows, bogs, wet ditches.*

140

Field Bindweed

×1¼

Convolvulus arvensis   June–September

The climbing or trailing stems frequently form thick mats. The leaves are about an inch to 2 inches long, variable in shape, but generally resemble blunt or sharp-pointed arrowheads. The flowers are an inch or less long and wide. The flower color is white but is very often weakly or strongly tinged with pink. *C. sepium* is also a climbing or trailing bindweed with triangular or heart-shaped leaves 2 to 4 inches long and white or pink flowers 1½ to 3 inches long and 2 to 3 inches across. Both of these species have been reported as mildly poisonous. Field Bindweed has also been called Creeping Jennie. *Fields, roadsides.*

141

Lady's Thumb

Polygonum persicaria   June–October

The erect or leaning stems are 8 inches to 3 feet tall with sheaths at each leaf stalk. The leaves are 3 to 6 inches long and tapered at both ends. Pale to dark pink flowers are in clusters about an inch long and ½ inch thick. There are many very similar species, but *P. sagittatum* and *P. arifolium* have stems with down-curving prickles, and the leaves of the former are smaller and elongate with rounded, backward-pointing lobes at the base, while the latter's leaves are larger and spearpoint-shaped with triangular basal lobes pointed outward. Lady's Thumb is poisonous and, interestingly, also bears the name Heart's Ease. *Moist or dry roadsides, fields, wood borders.*

142

Rose Pink

× ³⁄₄

Sabatia angularis   July–August

The stems are 4-angled and grow to a height of 8 inches to 3 feet. The paired, stalkless leaves are ½ inch to 2 inches long and ovate. The deep pink flowers have a yellow, star-shaped figure in the center. *S. brachiata* is a similar species but does not have angled stems. *S. paniculata* is also similar but has white flowers. *S. campanulata* and *S. stellaris* have unpaired stem branches, and the former has leaves that are widest near the base, while the latter's are widest near the tip. The flowers of *S. calycina* are pale pink or white with 5 to 7 petals. *S. dodecandra* has pink flowers with 6 to 13 petals. Rose Pink is also called Bitter Bloom. *Woods, fields, marshes.*

143

Marsh St. John's Wort

×2

Hypericum virginicum   July–August

This plant is 6 inches to 2 feet tall. The leaves are in pairs, oval or oblong, round-tipped, 1 to 2½ inches long, and their bases clasp the stem. The flowers are about ½ inch across and pale pink to deep pink or pinkish purple with a reddish center. A rare species of similar general appearance and habitat, *H. tubulosum*, has pink flowers about ¼ inch across and leaves 3 to 6 inches long that are narrowed at the base and do not clasp the stem. Several yellow-flowered species are cited with the description of *H. punctatum*. *Bogs, marshes.*

144

Seashore Mallow

×1

Kosteletzkya virginica   July–September

This plant is 2 to 3 feet tall. The leaves are heart-shaped and toothed, often have small, pointed lobes, and are 2 to 6 inches long. The flowers are 2 to 3 inches across and usually pink but may be purplish or almost white. The characteristics of this species are very similar to those of members of the genus *Hibiscus*, and some of these plants are cited in the descriptions of *H. moscheutos* and *H. trionum. Brackish marshes.*

Saltwort

× 1¼

Salsola kali   July–October

The striped stems of this plant are 8 inches to about 2 ½ feet tall and are often sprawling. The short, stiff, peglike leaves are ½ inch to 1 ½ inches long and tipped with a sharp spine. The flowers are about ½ inch across and vary in color from whitish or gray to yellowish gray or pink. Pink coloration of the flowers and pink to purple in the stems seem to be more evident later in the season. Saltwort is poisonous, and fragments of this prickly plant that become detached and fall to the sand can be hazardous to bare feet. Russian Thistle is another name for this species. *Sea beaches.*

Mistflower

×½

Eupatorium coelestinum July–October

The stems of this plant are hairy and grow from 1 to 3 feet tall. The leaves are in pairs, blunt-toothed on the margins, 1½ to 4 inches long, tapered to a point, and wrinkled. The small flowers are blue, violet, or purplish pink and grow in many clusters of 40 to 70 flowers at the ends of the stems. Another species, *E. incarnatum*, has pink flowers in clusters of only about 20, and the plant is often straggling and may be nearly 8 feet tall. Mistflower is also known as Ageratum. *Streamsides, wet woods and meadows.*

147

Dittany

Cunila origanoides

August–October

×2

The tufted stems are slender and 8 inches to about 1½ feet tall. The paired leaves are dark-dotted, about an inch to 1½ inches long, and stalkless or nearly so. The pale purple or pink flowers grow in small clusters from leaf bases or stem ends. Occasionally the flowers are almost white. The plant has been used as a remedy for chills and fever and for making a tealike beverage. Another common name for this plant is Stone Mint. *Open woods, rocky slopes.*

Elephant's-foot

× 1⅔

Elephantopus carolinianus   August–October

The branching stems are 6 inches to nearly 3 feet tall. Leaves are scattered along the stems and are 3 to 8 inches long, tapered at both ends, with rounded teeth along the margins. The pink or purplish flowers are less than ½ inch long and grow in several small leaf-bordered clusters. *E. tomentosus* and *E. nudatus* are similar species but have a cluster of larger leaves at ground level with much smaller leaves higher on the stem, and the former has leaves that are much softer to the touch. *Open woods.*

149

Scorpion Weed

×2

Phacelia dubia

March–May

This plant is 3 inches to about 1½ feet tall. The lower leaves are stalked and divided into several segments, while the upper leaves are usually smaller, almost stalkless, and lobed. The flowers are white, blue, or pinkish blue, about ½ inch across and hairy within. The flowers at first are arranged in a coil, which straightens as the flowers mature. This species often grows in attractive dense, many-flowered colonies. It is also commonly referred to by the name Phacelia. *Moist or dry woods, streamsides, clearings.*

Blue-eyed Grass

× ¾

Sisyrinchium angustifolium   March–June

The flattened stems of this plant grow in clumps 8 inches to almost 2 feet tall. The leaves are narrow and pointed, resembling those of grass. The flower color may be very pale blue to very dark blue. There are several species that are very similar. *S. atlanticum* and *S. arenicola* have branched stems, as does the species described here, but the first has very narrow stems, while the second has many old leaves present in the clump. *S. mucronatum* and *S. albidum* have unbranched stems and purple leaves just beneath the flowers, but the former has dark blue flowers, while the latter has pale blue or white flowers and usually wider stems and leaves. *Woods, thickets, meadows.*

Bird's Eye

× 1

Veronica persica   March–August

Many stems of this plant are prostrate. Oval, toothed leaves are paired except near flowers. Bright blue, pale-centered flowers are ½ inch across. Heart-shaped, hairy fruits are ½ inch wide. Other species are similar but with smaller flowers and fruits. Flowers of *V. agrestis* are solitary on long, slender stalks. Remaining species have elongate flower clusters on stalks bearing very small leaves. *V. arvensis* and *V. officinalis* grow in relatively dry places and are hairy, the former with minute flowers and erect stems, the latter with much larger leaves and prostrate stems. *V. americana* and *V. anagallis-aquatica* inhabit wet places, the former with stalked leaves, the latter with stalkless, clasping leaves. Speedwell is a common name applied to all species. *Roadsides, fields, lawns.*

Greater Periwinkle

Vinca major

×1¼

April–May

This plant usually has trailing stems but may stand 3 feet or more tall. The leaves are in pairs, dark green, and 1½ to 3 inches long. The leaves taper to a point from a rounded base or a squared-off base, and leaf margins have a fringe of small hairs. The flowers are 1½ to 2 inches across and blue to violet. *V. minor*, another very similar species, has flowers about an inch across and leaves smaller and without the hairy margin. These plants have escaped from cultivation after being introduced from Europe for ornamental planting. *Roadsides, wood borders.*

153

Bluets

× 1¼

Houstonia caerulea   April–June

The slender stems of this plant are 2 to 8 inches tall. There is a cluster of small leaves at the base of the stem, with pairs of even smaller leaves ½ inch or less in length up the stem. Flowers are solitary at the ends of the stems and vary in color from pale blue to pale purple, sometimes with a pinkish tint. The flower center is yellow. *H. patens* is similar but with darker purple flowers having dark reddish centers. *H. purpurea* has leaves as much as 2 inches long and ½ inch to 1¼ inches wide and clusters of pale purple to white flowers. Other species are cited with the description of *H. longifolia*. A second name for Bluets is Quaker Ladies. *Woods, fields, meadows, roadsides.*

Wild Lupine

$\times\,\frac{1}{4}$

Lupinus perennis   April–June

This plant is 6 inches to about 2 feet tall. The leaves are divided into several slender, pointed segments that are usually wider nearer the tip, and their arrangement at the tip of the leaf stalk gives a wheellike appearance. The flowers are blue, purplish blue, or occasionally white or pink and arranged in erect, elongate clusters 3 inches to nearly a foot long. The fruits are oblong, pointed, hairy pods an inch to 2 inches long. This species is said to be poisonous. The plants are sometimes found in fairly extensive colonies. *Roadsides, wood borders, open woods, clearings.*

Old Field Toadflax

Linaria canadensis

×2¼

April–September

The stems are very slender and smooth and 8 inches to about 2½ feet tall. There are usually shorter, flowerless stems sprawling at the base. The leaves are short and narrow, and those of the sprawling stems are in pairs or occasionally in circles. The flowers are about ½ inch long and are blue or purplish blue and white. There is a downward-pointing extension or spur from the lower end of the flower. *L. vulgaris* has very leafy stems and larger, yellow and orange flowers about an inch long in a dense cluster. *Roadsides, old fields.*

156

Blue Jasmine

×1¼

Clematis crispa   May–August

This plant is a climbing or sprawling vine. The leaves are in pairs along the stem and are divided into 3 to 5 segments that are narrowly to broadly oval with pointed or rounded tips. The flowers are pale blue, an inch to 2 inches long, and conspicuously flared. The margins of the flower parts are finely scalloped or wavy. A somewhat similar species, *C. viorna*, has purplish red flowers usually a little less than an inch long and much less noticeably flared. Another species is cited in the description of *C. virginiana*. Blue Jasmine is also called Leather Flower. *Wet woods, swamps.*

Rocket Larkspur

×⅔

Delphinium ajacis   May–September

The stems are about a foot to 3 feet tall, usually with some branching. The leaves are divided into several very narrow and pointed segments. The flowers are a little less than an inch to 1½ inches across and have a spur. Flower color is variable from pale to dark blue, purple, pink, or white. This larkspur is a European species that has been cultivated and has escaped into our native vegetation. It is frequently cited as a poisonous plant. *Roadsides, fields.*

Narrow-leaved Skullcap

× ½

Scutellaria integrifolia   June–July

The stems of this plant are hairy and 6 inches to more than
2½ feet tall. A few lower leaves may be stalked and oval in
shape, but the upper leaves are narrow, stalkless, an inch to
2½ inches long and about ¾ inch or less in width, and all
leaf margins are without teeth. The flowers are blue or bluish
pink and usually about an inch long with a hump or ridge on
the upper side of the base. Two other common species, *S.
lateriflora* and *S. elliptica*, are similar, but all the leaves are
toothed, and flowers of the former are only about ¼ inch
long, while the latter has more rounded leaves with blunt
tips. Narrow-leaved Skullcap is also known as Large-flowered
Skullcap. *Roadsides, wood borders, fields.*   159

Chicory × ½

Cichorium intybus   June–October

The stem is a foot to over 6 feet tall usually with many branches. The leaves at the base of the plant are about 4 inches to 1 foot long and have the margins toothed and lobed, while leaves in the upper part are very small, stalkless, and tend to clasp the stem. Many very small flowers in a dense cluster form what appears to be a single flower 1 inch or more across. The flower color is usually bright blue but may be white or infrequently pink. Extracts from Chicory give a desirable flavor to coffee, but the milk of cows that feed on the plant has an undesirable flavor. Blue Sailors is another name for this species. *Roadsides, fields.*

Pickerelweed

×⅔

Pontederia cordata   June–November

This plant grows to a height of a foot to 3 feet or more. The leaves are about 3 to 7 inches long, an inch to 4 inches wide, and heart-shaped. Occasionally leaves may be very slender. The flowers are dark blue in clusters 2 to 6 inches long and ½ inch to 1½ inches thick. Pickerelweed frequently forms thickly populated and extensive colonies. This species is occasionally called Tuckahoe. *Marshes, shallow water, wet banks of streams and ponds.*

161

Blue Cardinal Flower   × 1

Lobelia siphilitica   July–September

The thick stem of this mint is about a foot to about 5 feet
tall. The leaves are mostly 3 to 7 inches long, toothed,
pointed at both ends, and frequently wider near the tip.
Flowers are blue with white markings, about an inch long,
and develop in crowded clusters that may be over 1½ feet
long. *L. elongata* and *L. glandulosa* also have flowers about an
inch long, but the latter usually has few flowers and much
narrower leaves. The flowers of *L. puberula* are a bit smaller,
and the plant is covered with fine hairs. Other species are
cited in the description of *L. cardinalis*. Blue Cardinal Flower,
also called Great Lobelia, has been used medicinally, but
the active agents are poisonous. *Streamsides, wet woods and
meadows.*

162

Skunk Cabbage

× ⅔

Symplocarpus foetidus   February–April

There first appears a purple, mottled, hoodlike structure that is pointed and encloses the tiny flowers clustered on a fleshy stalk. The leaves develop after the flowers and may be as much as 2 feet long and over a foot wide. The plant has an unpleasant odor, as the name indicates, and there is a poisonous substance present. Even with the odor and the poison, Skunk Cabbage is said to be quite edible when properly cooked. *Swamps, wet woods and meadows.*

163

Liverwort

× ⅔

Hepatica americana   February–April

Stalks of leaves and flowers of this low plant arise directly from the ground. The leaf stalks are hairy, and the leaves are divided into 3 rounded lobes. The hairy flower stalks bear one flower that varies in color from white to pale or deep purple or pink-purple. There is another very similar species of the mountains, *H. acutiloba*, that has pointed leaf lobes. A belief that the shape of plant parts indicates that a similarly shaped part of the human body can be benefited by treatment with the plant assigned to Liverwort the status of a liver cure-all. This species is also called Round-lobed Liverleaf. *Wooded slopes, wood borders.*

Dwarf Iris

× 1⅔

Iris verna   March–May

This small iris is only 2 to 6 inches tall. The narrow, pointed leaves are 3 inches to over 1 foot long and overlap one another at their bases. The flowers are pale to dark purple with the outer segments marked with a central band of orange or yellow. *I. cristata*, a similar iris of the western border of the coastal plain, has a yellow to white ridge on the outer flower segments. *I. pseudoacorus* has yellow flowers. *I. prismatica* has blue-purple flowers and leaves usually less than ½ inch wide. *I. virginica* and *I. versicolor* have blue-purple flowers, but the former has a bright yellow spot on the outer flower segments, while the latter has a greenish yellow spot and conspicuous purple veining. Garden Iris, *Iris germanica*, escapes cultivation and has much larger flowers that may be blue, purple, yellow, or white. *Open sandy or rocky woods.*

165

Field Pansy

× 1½

Viola kitaibeliana   March–May

This violet has stems 2 inches to about a foot tall. The leaves are less than ½ inch to a little over an inch long, teardrop-shaped to round at the tip with narrow, fingerlike lobes at the base. The flowers are pale blue-purple often with a yellow center. The variation in flower color can range from white with blue veins to cream or pinkish blue. There are two other violets similar in general form. *V. arvensis* has yellow flowers, and is described herein. *V. tricolor* has some combination of yellow and purple floral color with the upper two petals usually darker. This latter species is one of those from which the cultivated pansy was developed. *Roadsides, fields, lawns.*

166

Bird-foot Violet

× ¾

Viola pedata   March–May

This apparently stemless violet has leaves and flowers growing
directly from the ground. The leaves are divided into several
oblong, narrow lobes, in turn often lobed or toothed and
wider near the tip. The flowers are an inch to nearly 2 inches
across and pale purple or lavender and often have the 2 upper
petals dark purple. The stamens make a spot of bright orange
in the center of the flower. Two other species, *V. brittoniana*
and *V. septemloba*, have divided, triangular leaves, and the
flowering stalks of the latter usually overtop the leaves. The
species *V. palmata* and *V. triloba* have divided leaves but are
hairy, and the latter usually has some leaves undivided. Bird-
foot Violet is also called Johnny-jump-up. *Rocky or sandy
woods, roadsides.*

167

Jack-in-the-pulpit

× ¾

Arisaema triphyllum   March–June

This plant grows from 6 inches to almost 3 feet tall. The leaves are on long stalks and divided into 3 large segments 3 to 8 inches long and tapered at both ends. Often only 1 leaf develops. The very small flowers grow on the base of a stalk, Jack, that may be greenish, yellowish, or purple, and the stalk is enclosed by a hooded leaf, the pulpit, that is green, white, or purple and either striped or unstriped. The fruits develop as a large cluster of bright red berries. *A. dracontium* has 5 to 15 leaf segments, and Jack is much longer than the pulpit. Jack-in-the-pulpit is poisonous but when properly cooked is edible. Another name is Indian Turnip. *Wet woods, swamps.*

Common Vetch

Vicia angustifolia   March–June

The stems are sprawling and 6 inches to about 3 feet long.
The leaves are divided into 3 to 5 pairs of oblong segments
with a small spine at the tip. The pinkish purple, stalkless
flowers are usually in pairs at the base of the upper leaf stalks.
V. sativa is very similar but has dark blue or purple petals on
its flowers and usually 4 to 8 pairs of leaf segments. *V.
grandiflora* has pale yellow flowers. *V. caroliniana* has distinct
flower stalks and pale blue to white flowers in an elongate
cluster. Other species are cited with the description of *V.
dasycarpa. Roadsides, fields.*

169

Purple Dead Nettle $\times 1\frac{1}{2}$

Lamium purpureum March–August

The stems are square and 3 inches to over 1½ feet tall. The paired, heart-shaped leaves are toothed and have a wrinkled appearance; also, many of the upper leaves are reddish purple. The flowers are reddish purple to dark, dull red and grow in small clusters toward the end of the stem. A similar species, *L. amplexicaule*, with stalkless upper leaves is described herein. Plants that are referred to as nettles usually have stinging hairs, but this is not the case with either of these species. *Roadsides, fields, lawns.*

170

Henbit

× 1½

Lamium amplexicaule   March–October

The square stems of this plant stand 4 inches to over a foot tall with low branches spreading close to the ground. The paired, often nearly round leaves are scalloped and about ½ inch to 1½ inches across, with the lower leaves long-stalked and the upper almost stalkless. The pinkish purple flowers may range from pink to reddish purple and grow in clusters just above a pair of stalkless leaves. Another species, *L. purpureum*, is included here. Dead Nettle is another common name for Henbit. *Roadsides, fields, lawns.*

171

Cancer Weed

× ½

Salvia lyrata   April–June

The usually leafless stalk of this plant is a foot to 2 feet tall. All or most of the leaves are at ground level and generally deeply lobed with the lobe at the tip much larger. The flowers are pale to dark purple or blue and are clustered in circles that are spaced apart on the upper part of the flowering stalk. *S. urticifolia* has pale or dark blue and white flowers and has unlobed, toothed leaves up the stem that are oval to triangular. *S. splendens* is the Scarlet Sage that is so often cultivated. Cancer Weed, also a sage, is known by a second name, Lyre-leaved Sage. *Roadsides, fields, open woods.*

Spiderwort

× 1

Tradescantia ohiensis   April–June

This plant is about ½ foot to over 3 feet tall. The grasslike leaves are frequently a foot to over 3 feet long, very narrow, and folded, their bases sheathing the stem. Usually the leaves have a whitish coating that rubs off. The flowers are about ½ to 1 inch across and range in color from purple to blue or pinkish blue. *T. virginiana* is a very similar species; however, the flowers are usually purple or blue-purple, the leaves lack the whitish coating, and the green segments on the underside of the flower are densely hairy. *T. rosea* has extremely narrow leaves and bright pink flowers. These plants are sometimes cultivated for ornament. *Wood borders, roadsides, meadows.*

173

Vetchling

Lathyrus venosus   May–July

The stems of this sprawling plant are 4-angled and sometimes very hairy. The leaves are divided into 8 to 12 segments that are tapered at both ends, usually rounded at the tip, and have a curling tendril. Flowers are about an inch long, purple or purple with some white, and usually in clusters of 5 to 20. Fruits are pods 1½ to 2½ inches long. *L. palustris* is a similar species but has only 4 to 6 leaf segments and usually only 2 to 6 flowers in a cluster. *L. latifolius* has only 2 leaf segments ½ inch to a little more than an inch wide and flowering stalks 4 to 8 inches long. *L. hirsutus* also has 2 leaf segments, but they are usually less than ½ inch wide, and the flowering stalks are only 1½ to 4 inches long. Wild Pea is another name for the vetchlings. *Moist to dry woods, thickets.*

174

Nightshade

Solanum dulcamara   May–September

This vine may climb or trail along the ground. The leaves are heart-shaped, often with lobes at the base, and 2½ to 4 inches long. Bruised leaves have an unpleasant odor. Flowers are about ½ to 1 inch across and vary from dark blue to purple or rarely white. The fruit is oval, bright red, and about ½ inch long. *S. nigrum* and *S. americanum* are variable in foliage and have similar flower structures, but the flowers are pale purple or white developing into black fruits; fruits of the latter are glossy. *S. dulcamara* and *S. nigrum* are European introductions that are poisonous; yet the ripe fruits are said to be edible when cooked. Nightshade also goes by the name Bittersweet. *Roadsides, thickets, stream banks.*   175

Smooth Vetch

× 1¼

Vicia dasycarpa   May–September

The stems are 1½ to 3 feet long and trailing or climbing. The leaves are divided into several oblong segments and have curling tendrils at the tip. Flowers are in clusters of 10 to 20, about an inch long and partly dark purple and partly pale purple or white, with the bases appearing swollen. *V. villosa* is very similar but has very hairy stems and leaves and flowers in clusters of 10 to 40. *V. cracca* has blue-violet flowers in clusters of 20 to 50 without swollen bases. *V. hirsuta* has pale purple flowers only ½ inch long or less in clusters of 4 or 5. Other species are cited in the description of *V. angustifolia*. *Roadsides, fields.*

176

Wild Garlic

Allium ampeloprasum

× ⅓

June

The stems of this plant are usually about 3 feet tall. The leaves are long and narrow, and their bases sheath the stem. The small dark purple flowers are arranged in a dense, rounded mass 2 to 3 inches across. An additional species is cited in the description of *A. canadense*. This plant, known locally as Yorktown Onion, was introduced from England during the early days of the country and found a home in the area that is now York County where it sometimes forms fairly extensive colonies. *Roadsides, fields.*

177

False Dragonhead

Physostegia denticulata

June–July

The stems of this plant reach 1½ to 3½ feet. The paired leaves are 2 to 6 inches long with short, blunt teeth, stalkless except for the lower ones, and usually wider near the tip. The purple or white flowers are ½ to ¾ inch long. A similar species, *P. virginiana*, is a frequently cultivated species that escapes from gardens and has the flowers close together on the stalk and leaves with sharp, curved teeth. Obedient Plant is another name for these plants, for the flowers, when moved, will remain in the new position. *Wet ditches, marshes, low roadsides, swamp borders.*

Common Milkweed

× ½

Asclepias syriaca   June–August

This milkweed often has stems nearly 6 feet tall. The leaves are in pairs, thick-stalked, and 5 to 10 inches long. The flowers are pale or dull purple varying to greenish or pinkish purple, and the clusters of flowers are usually numerous. The fruit is a pointed pod 3 to 5 inches long covered with stout spines, an excellent identifying feature. *A amplexicaulis* has stalkless, wavy-margined leaves. *A. purpurascens* has deep purple flowers often in 1 or very few clusters and stems a foot to 3 feet tall. Other species are cited with the description of *A. variegata*. Common Milkweed has been reported as being poisonous, although the ripe fruits and young stems and leaves have been used as food when cooked. *Roadsides, fields.*   179

Common Motherwort

× ⅔

Leonurus cardiaca   June–August

The square stems of this tall plant may reach a height of about 5 feet. The paired leaves are 2 to 5 inches long and divided into 3 to 5 sharply toothed lobes. The leaves on the upper part of the stem are smaller and usually end in 3 large teeth. The pale purple or pink-purple flowers are hairy, and the basal portion is somewhat prickly. The flowers are clustered closely around the stem. This plant was once cultivated in its native Europe for supposed medicinal value and is now reported to cause skin inflammation when handled. *Roadsides, woodland trails.*

Butterfly Pea

× 1¼

Clitoria mariana   June–August

This is a trailing or twining plant with stems as much as 3
feet long. The leaves are divided into 3 segments an inch to
3 inches long and oval or oblong with the widest part often
nearer the base. The flower is about 2 inches long and pale
blue to pale pinkish purple. The fruit is a flattened pod an
inch to 2½ inches long and pointed at both ends. *Centrosema
virginianum* is a very similar plant but has a projection or spur
on the back of the flower at the base, and the fruit is 3 to 5½
inches long. Both of these species are called by the same
common name. *Dry and open woods, wood borders, clearings.*   181

Blue Vervain

× ½

Verbena hastata   June–September

The stems of this plant are 2 to 5 feet tall and are usually much branched near the top. The leaves are in pairs, 2 to 8 inches long, toothed, taper to a point, and are sometimes lobed near the base. The slender, pointed, erect flowering spikes are usually numerous near the top of the stems and have a few of the purple to pink flowers encircling the spikes. Deeply lobed leaves distinguish another species, *V. officinalis*, and flowering spikes less than 2 inches long mark *V. brasiliensis*. Of 3 species having flowers more spaced apart, *V. urticifolia* has white flowers, *V. simplex* has leaves less than ½ inch wide, and *V. scabra* has very rough stems. Blue Vervain was supposed to have curative properties; thus its status as a medicinal plant, or simple, brought the name Simpler's Joy. *Moist fields, thickets, swamps.*

Monkey Flower

×2

Mimulus ringens   June–September

The square stems of this plant grow to a height of 2 to over
4 feet. The paired, toothed leaves have no stalks, are 2 to 5
inches long, and taper to a rounded or pointed tip. The
flower color varies from deep to pale purple to almost white.
M. alatus is a very similar species in general appearance and
flower color and form, but the leaves are stalked, and the
stems are winged. *Bogs, marshes, wet meadows, streamsides.*

183

Cross Milkwort

× 1

Polygala cruciata   June–September

This plant is 4 to 15 inches tall. Leaves are narrow, ½ inch
to 1½ inches long, wider near the tip, and grow in circles of
4. The flowers clustered at the ends of the stems are dark to
pale pinkish purple or greenish purple. One other species, *P.
verticillata*, has circled leaves but slender, pointed flower clusters. Except for noncircled leaves *P. sanguinea* is very similar
to the pictured plant. *P. incarnata* has a whitish coating and
deep pink, fringed flowers. *P. nuttallii* has flowering clusters
only ½ inch long and ¼ inch thick and very short, narrow
leaves. Other species are cited with the description of *P. lutea*.
Cross Milkwort is also known as Drum-heads. *Bogs, marshes,
wet meadows.*

Passion Flower × 1½

Passiflora incarnata   June–September

This plant is a trailing or climbing vine. The leaves are divided into 3 lobes that are pointed, toothed, and 2 to 6 inches long. The unusually structured flower is a combination of white, bluish, pink-purple, and purple. The oval fruits are greenish yellow and are edible. The various parts of the floral structure have been interpreted as symbolic of elements of the Crucifixion. The name Maypops has been applied to this plant. Another species, *P. lutea*, has smaller, yellow flowers and is included. *Fields, roadsides, thickets.*

Ruellia

×1

Ruellia caroliniensis   June–September

The height of the plant is 6 inches to about 3 feet. The stems
are usually hairy. The paired leaves are 2 to 5 inches long,
tapered at both ends or sometimes rounded at 1 or both ends,
and are usually crowded toward the tip of the stem. The
flowers are an inch to 2 inches long and an inch to almost 2
inches across; they are clustered in the upper half of the plant
and may be purple, pinkish blue, or blue. *R. humilis* and *R.
streptens* occur less frequently; the former has stalkless or very
short-stalked leaves, while the latter has flowers about an
inch to 2½ inches long clustered in the upper half of the
plant or solitary about the middle. *Open woods, roadsides,
fields.*

186

Purple Loosestrife

× ½

Lythrum salicaria   June–September

The plant is about 2 to nearly 6 feet tall. The leaves are in pairs or circles, an inch to 4 inches long, ¼ to almost an inch wide, and taper gradually to a point. The flowers are reddish purple and grow in clusters 6 inches to over a foot long. Careful examination of the flowers shows that there are 3 kinds that vary in structure with respect to the positions of the parts producing and the parts receiving pollen. *L. lanceolatum* has many leaves single rather than in pairs and only 2 kinds of flower structure. *L. lineare* also has 2 kinds of floral structure, but the flowers are violet or white, and the leaves are less than 2 inches long and less than ¼ inch wide. Purple Loosestrife, also called Spiked Loosestrife, is a native of Europe that has spread rapidly from cultivation. *Marshes, wet meadows, streamsides.*

Musk Thistle × ⅔

Carduus nutans June–October

This plant is usually 2 to 5 feet tall but may be much taller. The stems and leaves are very prickly. The leaves are 5 inches to over a foot long and have spiny tips and lobes. The spiny-based flower heads are 1½ to 3 inches across, purple, and usually nodding. There are 4 similar species in the genus *Cirsium*. *C. vulgare* has conspicuously spiny wings on the stem from leaf to leaf. *C. discolor* has a feltlike coat of white hairs on the undersides of the leaves. *C. repandum* has very crowded, wavy-margined leaves and *C. nuttallii* has pink or white flowers. Musk Thistle is also called Nodding Thistle.

Roadsides, fields.

Groundnut

Apios americana   July–August

The twining and climbing stems are 2 to 10 feet long. The leaves are 4 to 8 inches long and are divided into usually 4 to 7 segments that are an inch to 2½ inches long and taper from a rounded base to a point. The brownish to reddish purple flowers are about ½ inch long and grow in dense clusters 2 to 6 inches long. The fruit is a pod 2 to 5 inches long. The underground stems and seeds are edible when properly cooked and are said to have furnished food for the American Indians and early settlers. Indian Potato is another name for Groundnut. *Rich woods, moist thickets.*

189

Teasel

Dipsacus sylvestris   July–September

The prickly stems of Teasel are 2 to 9 feet tall. The leaves are also prickly and grow in pairs; the bases of many are fused around the stem. The small flowers are about ½ inch long and develop from the middle toward the end of an oval-shaped head 2 to 4 inches long. Flower color varies from pale blue-pink to purple or white. The dense flower cluster grows in a mass of slender spines. Teasel is a European introduction that is well established in our flora. The spiny flower heads have been used in teasing fabrics and are a part of many ornamental dried arrangements. *Roadsides, fields, pastures.*

Ironweed

× ¾

Vernonia noveboracensis   July–September

This plant is 3 to 7 feet tall. The leaves are 4 to 10 inches long, taper to a point at both ends, and have few to many small teeth on the margins. The arrangement of flower clusters is greatly widened in the upper part and is usually flat-topped. The flowers are purple but usually appear pink in photographs. *V. glauca* is an extremely similar species with pale green or whitish undersides of the leaves. *Wet woods, marshes, meadows, streamsides.*

Ivyleaf Morning Glory

× 1

Ipomoea hederacea   July–October

The hairy, twining stems of this plant may climb to a height of 3 to 6 feet. The leaves are also hairy, 2 to 5 inches long and about as wide, and divided into 3 pointed lobes. The flower is about an inch to 2 inches long and blue or purple usually with a white center. Another somewhat similar species, *I. lacunosa*, has few or no hairs on stems and leaves, heart-shaped leaves or 3-lobed leaves, and white flowers ½ to an inch long. Other species are cited in the descriptions of *I. pandurata* and *I. coccinea*. *Roadsides, fields, wood borders.*

Common Burdock

×2

Arctium minus   July–October

The stems of this plant are 2 to 5 feet tall and usually have many branches. The leaves are oval or heart-shaped and may be over 1 ½ feet long and about a foot wide. The leaf stalks are usually hollow. The small reddish purple or purplish pink flowers grow in compact, roundish clusters enclosed by a burrlike head of spines ½ to about an inch across on very short stalks. Common Burdock is also called Clotbur. *Road-sides, fields, pastures.*

Clammy Waxweed

Cuphea petiolata

× 2¼

July–October

The stems are usually 6 inches to a foot tall but may be taller, and they are purplish or reddish and covered with sticky hairs. The leaves are about an inch to 2 inches long, long-stalked, and in pairs. The purple flowers are about ½ inch long, and 2 upper petals are larger than the other 4. The base of the flower is enlarged or bulbous on the upper side. This plant is known also by the name Blue Waxweed. *Roadsides, fields, pastures, meadows.*

Water Hemp

Acnida cannabina   July–October

× ½

The stout stems of this plant may be an inch or more in diameter near the ground and may reach a height of nearly 8 feet. The leaves are 3 to 8 inches long, relatively narrow, long-stalked, and taper gradually toward both ends. The tiny flowers are densely clustered in numerous slender spires that are green to greenish purple or reddish purple. Two similar species, *A. hybridus* and *A. retroflexus*, grow in drier ground, and the former has many leaves more oval and short-pointed, while the latter has many leaves somewhat triangular and thicker flowering clusters. *A. spinosus* is a much smaller plant with spiny stems. Marijuana, also called Hemp, is *Cannabis sativa. Salt and brackish marshes.*

Gerardia

× 1¼

Gerardia purpurea   August–September

This plant is about a foot to 4 feet tall with spreading branches that are somewhat rough to the touch. The narrow, paired leaves are ½ inch to 1½ inches long. The flowers are an inch or more across and purple with yellow lines and darker purple spots within. *G. racemulosa* is a similar species but has erect, smooth branches and slightly smaller flowers. *G. maritima*, a plant of salt marshes, is often purplish and usually has thicker leaves. *G. tenuifolia* and *G. setacea* are plants of dry soils, and the former has flowers with the 2 upper lobes longer than the lower and directed forward, while the latter has the upper 2 flower lobes erect and densely hairy within. Yellow-flowered species are cited in the description of *G. pedicularia*. *Moist, open woods and roadsides, streamsides, meadows.*

Marsh Fleabane

× 1¼

Pluchea purpurascens   August–October

This plant is a foot to over 4 feet tall. The leaves have very short stalks frequently winged by the extension of the lower part of the leaf blade, have few to many teeth on the margins, taper to a pointed or rounded tip, and are 2 to 6 inches long. The tiny flowers are arranged in very dense clusters each resembling a single flower, and many of these clusters together form a flat-topped pinkish purple group at the stem ends. *P. camphorata* and *P. foetida* are similar species, but the former has definitely stalked leaves, and the latter has an unpleasant odor as well as leaves that enclose or clasp the stem. *Brackish marshes.*

Purplestem Aster

× ¾

Aster puniceus   August–October

This aster is a foot to about 8 feet tall with usually hairy, purplish stems. Leaves are highly variable but usually are stalkless and clasp the stem. Flower heads are about 2 inches across and have blue to deep purple bordering flowers and yellow to red central ones. Other similar species are also found in moist places. *A. gracilis* has leaves about ½ inch wide or less and only 9 to 15 blue or violet bordering flowers. *A. tenuifolius* has leaves ¼ inch wide or less and 15 to 25 white to pale purple bordering flowers. *A. simplex* and *A. novi-belgii* have leaves an inch or more wide, and the former has usually white bordering flowers, while the latter usually has blue to violet bordering flowers. *Wet woods and meadows, marshes.*

Beautyberry × ½

Callicarpa americana August–October

This shrub is 1½ to 6 feet tall. The stems are hairy and usually have many branches. The leaves are in pairs, 3 to 8 inches long, long-stalked, and toothed. Flowers are small, about ¼ inch long and wide, and vary in color from very pale pink to blue. The dense flower clusters are located at the bases of the leaves and are shorter than the leaf stalks. The fruits are the most conspicuous feature of the plant and are reddish pink to reddish purple. A rare species, *C. dichotoma*, is similar but has smaller leaves and flower clusters on stalks longer than the leaf stalks. These species are sometimes cultivated as ornamentals. Beautyberry is also known as French Mulberry. *Moist woods and wood borders.*

199

Blazing Star

× 1

Liatris graminifolia   September–October

The stems stand a foot to almost 5 feet tall. The numerous
leaves are grasslike, narrow and pointed, and the larger ones
near the ground are as much as a foot long and only about ½
inch or less wide. The purple to pink-purple flowers are in
clusters resembling single flowers that form larger, elongate
clusters at the ends of the stems. In *L. squarrosa* the bases of
the flowerlike clusters have the green or purplish green segments curved outward. *L. scariosa* has lower leaves an inch to
2 inches wide, and the stalks of the flowerlike clusters are ½
to over 2 inches long. *L. spicata* has flowerlike clusters without stalks, and the larger, elongate clusters at the stem ends
are very densely crowded. *Open woods, roadside banks, fields.*

Index of Families and Pronunciation Key

The symbols ˋ and ´ mark the syllable to be accented; the former calls for a long vowel sound, while the latter calls for a short vowel sound.

Acanthàceae
  Ruéllia caroliniénsis
Alismatàceae
  Sagittària latifòlia
Amaranthàceae
  Acnìda cannábina
  Alternanthèra philoxeroìdes
Amaryllidàceae
  Hypóxis hirsùta
  Zephránthes atamásco
Apocynàceae
  Vínca màjor
Aràceae
  Arisaèma triphýllum
  Oróntium aquáticum
  Symplocárpus foètidus
Araliàceae
  Pànax quinquefòlius
Asclepiadàceae
  Asclèpias lanceolàta
  Asclèpias syrìaca
  Asclèpias tuberòsa
  Asclèpias variegàta
Balsaminàceae
  Impàtiens capénsis
Berberidàceae
  Podophýllum peltàtum
Bignoniàceae
  Bignònia capreolàta
Campanulàceae
  Lobèlia cardinàlis
  Lobèlia siphilítica
Caprifoliàceae
  Lonícera japónica
Caryophyllàceae
  Agrostémma githàgo
  Lýchnis álba
  Lýchnis coronària
  Silène caroliniàna
  Silène cucùbalus
Chenopodiàceae
  Sálsola kàli
Commelinàceae

Tradescántia ohiénsis
Compósitae
  Árctium mínus
  Áster puníceus
  Cárduus nùtans
  Chrysógonum virginiànum
  Cichòrium íntybus
  Círsium horrídulum
  Coreópsis lanceolàta
  Coreópsis tinctòria
  Elephántopus caroliniànus
  Erígeron pulchéllus
  Erígeron strigòsus
  Eupatòrium coelestìnum
  Helénium nudiflòrum
  Helénium tenuifòlium
  Hieràcium praténse
  Hypochoèris radicàta
  Krígia virgínica
  Liàtris graminifòlia
  Plùchea purpuráscens
  Rudbéckia tríloba
  Senécio aùreus
  Sericocárpus asteroìdes
  Solidàgo bícolor
  Solidàgo caèsia
  Solidàgo júncea
  Sónchus ásper
  Vernònia noveboracénsis
Convolvulàceae
  Convólvulus arvénsis
  Ipomoèa coccínea
  Ipomoèa hederàcea
  Ipomoèa panduràta
Crucíferae
  Cardámine bulbòsa
  Ráphanus raphanístrum
Cyperàceae
  Cypèrus retrofráctus
  Dichròmena coloràta
  Erióphorum virgínicum
Dipsacàceae
  Dípsacus sylvéstris

Droseràceae
Drósera rotundifòlia
Ericàceae
Epigaèa rèpens
Gaulthèria procúmbens
Rhododéndron nudiflòrum
Vaccínium macrocárpon
Zenòbia pulverulénta
Euphorbiàceae
Cnidóscolus stimulòsus
Euphórbia cyparíssias
Euphórbia heterophýlla
Euphórbia marginàta
Gentianàceae
Sabàtia angulàris
Geraniàceae
Gerànium mólle
Gramíneae
Cénchrus tribuloìdes
Uníola paniculàta
Guttíferae
Hyperìcum punctàtum
Hyperìcum virgínicum
Hydrophyllàceae
Phacèlia dùbia
Iridàceae
Belamcánda chinénsis
Ìris vérna
Sisyrínchium angustifòlium
Labiàtae
Collinsónia canadénsis
Cunìla origanoìdes
Làmium amplexicaùle
Làmium purpùreum
Leonùrus cardìaca
Physostégia denticulàta
Sálvia lyràta
Scutellària integrifòlia
Leguminòsae
Àpios americàna
Cássia fasciculàta
Clitòria mariàna
Láthyrus venòsus
Lòtus corniculàtus
Lupìnus perénnis
Melilòtus álba
Stylosánthes biflòra
Tephròsia spicàta
Trifòlium arvénse
Trifòlium procúmbens
Vícia angustifòlia
Vícia dasycárpa
Liliàceae

Állium ampelopràsum
Állium canadénse
Chamaèlirium lùteum
Helònias bullàta
Lílium supérbum
Medèola virginiàna
Ornithógalum umbellàtum
Polygónatum biflòrum
Tríllium pusíllum
Uvulària sessilifòlia
Linàceae
Lìnum mèdium
Loganiàceae
Gelsèmium sempérvirens
Lythràceae
Cùphea petiolàta
Lýthrum salicària
Malvàceae
Hibíscus moscheùtos
Hibíscus triònum
Kostelétzkya virgínica
Modìola caroliniàna
Melastomatàceae
Rhéxia virgínica
Nymphaeàceae
Nùphar ádvena
Nymphaèa odoràta
Onagràceae
Gaùra biénnis
Oenothèra laciniàta
Orchidàceae
Cypripèdium acaùle
Cypripèdium calcèolus
Goodyèra pubéscens
Habenària ciliàris
Habenària clavellàta
Habenària lácera
Órchis spectábilis
Pogònia ophioglossoìdes
Ponthièva racemòsa
Spiránthes vernàlis
Orobanchàceae
Conópholis americàna
Oxalidàceae
Óxalis rùbra
Óxalis strícta
Papaveràceae
Corýdalis flàvula
Fumària officinàlis
Papàver dùbium
Sanguinària canadénsis
Passifloràceae
Passiflòra incarnàta

Passiflòra lùtea
Phytolaccàceae
   Phytolácca americàna
Plantaginàceae
   Plantàgo lanceolàta
Polemoniàceae
   Phlóx drummóndii
   Phlóx subulàta
Polygalàceae
   Polýgala cruciàta
   Polýgala lùtea
Polygonàceae
   Polýgonum persicària
Pontederiàceae
   Heteranthèra dùbia
   Pontedèria cordàta
Portulacàceae
   Claytònia virgínica
Primulàceae
   Lysimàchia ciliàta
   Lysimàchia nummulària
Pyrolàceae
   Monótropa hypópithys
Ranunculàceae
   Anemòne quinquefòlia
   Anemòne virginiàna
   Aquilègia canadénsis
   Cáltha palústris
   Clématis críspa
   Clématis virginiàna
   Delphínium ajàcis
   Hepática americàna
   Ranùnculus híspidus
Rosàceae
   Duchésnea índica
   Potentílla canadénsis
   Rùbus phoenicolàsius
Rubiàceae

Houstònia caerùlea
Houstònia longifòlia
Mitchélla rèpens
Sherárdia arvénsis
Sarraceniàceae
   Sarracènia flàva
Saururàceae
   Saurùrus cérnuus
Saxifragàceae
   Parnássia asarifòlia
Scrophulariàceae
   Chelòne glàbra
   Gerárdia pediculària
   Gerárdia purpùrea
   Linària canadénsis
   Mímulus ríngens
   Verónica pérsica
   Veronicástrum virgínicum
Solanàceae
   Phýsalis heterophýlla
   Solànum dulcamàra
Umbellíferae
   Conìum maculàtum
   Foenículum vulgàre
   Hydrocótyle verticillàta
   Tháspium barbinòde
Valerianàceae
   Valerianélla radiàta
Verbenàceae
   Callicárpa americàna
   Verbèna hastàta
Violàceae
   Vìola arvénsis
   Vìola kitaibeliàna
   Vìola pedàta
Vitàceae
   Parthenocíssus quinquefòlia

Index of Common and Scientific Names